ONE HEART FULL OF LOVE

One Heart Full of Love

Mother Teresa

Edited by José Luis González-Balado

Collins
FOUNT PAPERBACKS

First published in Spanish as *Seremos juzgados sobre el AMOR*
by Ediciones Paulinas of Madrid in 1984

English edition first published in the United States of America
in 1988 by Servant Books of Ann Arbor, Michigan

This edition first published in Great Britain
in 1989 by Fount Paperbacks, London

Printed and bound in Great Britain by
William Collins Sons & Co. Ltd, Glasgow.

This collection of addresses, interviews, comments, and
a letter by Agnes Bojaxhiu – known as Mother Teresa of
Calcutta – was edited by José Luis Gonzáles-Balado and
originally published in Spanish by Ediciones Paulinas.
This English-language edition of the work was translated
from Spanish into English by Susana Labastida.

Table of Contents

Publisher's Preface

THIS BOOK IS A COLLECTION of some of the addresses, interviews, comments, and correspondence of Agnes Bojaxhiu, who is known and loved by millions as Mother Teresa of Calcutta, the founder of the Missionaries of Charity. Most of the addresses and interviews center on the inspiring call to love others unconditionally with the love of Jesus Christ, especially those most in need in our own families and neighborhoods, and on our own city streets. The material has been edited by José Luis González-Balado and was originally published in Spanish.

In this work, each address or interview of Mother Teresa has been treated as a separate chapter. The origin of the material in each chapter—whether it is an address or interview (including one letter and one selection of comments)—is cited at the bottom of the first page of the chapter. Other notes, which are numbered in the text, have been organized by chapter and placed in an appendix.

The reader should note that Mother Teresa rarely quotes from Scripture directly or cites references when she speaks before an audience. Yet her paraphrases of Scripture and other works remain true to the meaning of the original text. Frequently, the paraphrases are taken from oft-quoted texts that will be familiar to the reader.

Further, the reader should note that Mother Teresa often uses the same examples or illustrations in her addresses and interviews. But she always tailors them to suit the topic, the audience, and the occasion—many times rendering an already familiar illustration with fresh insight and meaning.

Finally, the meaning of Mother Teresa's statements should be considered carefully by the reader. The context for her statements is always an unflagging commitment to Jesus Christ and his church, along with her special mission to serve the poorest of the poor. Without that understanding, the reader may, at times, misconstrue the meaning of her simple and forthright statements about serving Christ in the poor or some other critical issue, such as care of the elderly. The reader will find some of the chapter notes helpful in clarifying the meaning of particular statements.

As you read this book, it is our sincere prayer that the simple yet profound words of Mother Teresa may enkindle the fire of God's love in your heart, especially for those most in need in your midst.

ONE

We Will Be Judged by Our Love

I am deeply grateful to God for allowing me to share with you, so I can bring you the joy and gratitude of our people, the poor, under whose distressing appearance Christ is hidden. You possess a wonderful and noble goal: to try to find ways of putting into practice your love for God and for your neighbor. Faith in action is love, and love in action is service. By transforming that faith into living acts of love, we put ourselves in contact with God himself, with Jesus our Lord.

Giving and Self-Giving

Some time ago a Hindu gentleman was asked, "What is a Christian?" He gave an answer that was both very simple and surprising. "A Christian is someone who gives of himself." From the very start, we

This talk was given by Mother Teresa at the LaSallian Federation World Convention of Christian School Alumni in Malta on August 30, 1976.

perceive that indeed to be a Christian is nothing other than to give of oneself for the sake of Christ. God so loved the world that he gave us his Son. That was the first act of self-giving. His Son was given to us because he wanted to be one with us, like us in everything except sin.

The Son's coming is ushered in by a new act of self-giving. Christ is given into the care of a woman, the Blessed Virgin Mary, the virgin immaculate. Because of her deep humility and total openness to God, the first thing that occurs to Mary is to share her son with others.

With the attitude of a servant of the Lord, Mary went with haste to share Jesus with others. We know what happened when St. John the Baptist welcomed Jesus while he was still in the womb. Mary's gift of Jesus filled St. John and his parents with joy when the virgin arrived pregnant with child to visit her cousin Elizabeth.

As if this self-giving, this first self-giving, were not enough, Christ made himself the Bread of Life. He wanted to give himself to us in a very special way—in a simple, tangible way—because it is hard for human beings to love God whom they cannot see. He made himself the Bread of Life to satisfy our love for God, our hunger for God. We have been created for greater things. We have been created in God's image and likeness. We have been created to love and to be loved.

The Bread of Life

Jesus put a condition on his self-giving: "If you do not eat my flesh and drink my blood, you will have no life in you. You will be unable to love or to give." The condition is very simple and clear, even a child is able to eat bread. Bread is the simplest food for people everywhere, and it is usually the cheapest. Well, then, Christ became the Bread of Life.

But it seems that this act of self-giving wasn't enough for him. He wanted to give something more. He wanted to pass on to us the opportunity to give of ourselves to him, so we could turn our love for him into living deeds after eating the Bread of Life. To accomplish that, he became the hungry one, the naked one, stripped of all earthly goods and comforts. Christ says: "For I was hungry and you gave me to eat. I was homeless and you offered me shelter. I was illiterate and you taught me to read. I was alone and you kept me company. You gave me your understanding and your love."[1]

Christ made this kind of total self-giving a condition for life. He will judge us at the hour of our death. We will be judged by what we have done, by what we have been, to the poor. He says to us: "I was hungry and you did not feed me. I hungered for bread, for justice, and for human dignity; yet you passed me by! I was naked and stripped of every necessity, denied justice and even the simple recognition that I am just like you, created by the same loving God to love and to be loved. But I was left for dead, alone and dejected. I was thrown out into the streets, unwanted, unloved, and ignored.

The lepers, the blind, the invalid, and the handi-capped are asking if you notice them, if you recognize them in your midst. This is the reason why I am speaking to you. You need to become aware of these people and their needs. Do you know them?

Knowing the Poor

This is why I speak to you, so you can become aware of these people who are calling out to you. Does each one of you, before anything else, know the poor in your homes? Are you aware that in your own family, in your own living situation, there may be someone who is very lonely, who feels unloved or hurt? Are you aware of this? Maybe that lonely or hurt one is your own husband, your wife or your child, who is lonely at home, in the same home where you live. Are you aware of that?

Where are our elderly today? Many are in nursing homes.[2] Why? Many times it is because no one wants them, because they have become a burden.

I remember very vividly some time ago when I visited a magnificent nursing home for the elderly. It had everything you could want, beautiful things. There were about forty patients there, and they apparently had all of their material and medical needs met. But everybody was looking toward the door. I did not see a single person with a smile on his or her face. I turned to the sister who was on duty, and I asked, "Sister, how is that? How is it that these people who have everything here, are all looking toward the door?" The sister answered my question frankly, "It happens nearly every day. They are expecting and hoping that a son or a daughter will come to visit them. They are hurt because they are forgotten. They always say, 'Maybe my son or my daughter, someone from my family, or one of my friends will come to see me.'" This is real poverty.

I remember one time when I pulled a woman, who

knew that she was dying, out of a trash heap. I pulled her out and took her to our home for the dying. She kept on saying the same thing over and over, "My son has done this to me!" I didn't hear her cry out, "I'm hungry! I'm dying! I can't stand the pain!" No, she kept saying, "My son has done this to me!" It took me a long time to help her finally say, "I forgive my son." I got her to say these words when she was at the very point of dying.

Not Pity but Love

That is poverty. Do you realize that? Does that kind of poverty exist in your own home, among your own neighbors, at the place where you work, or among any of the people with whom you have regular contact? Do you know them well? Do they know you? That is something that the Hindu gentleman I mentioned earlier knew how to express in a very beautiful way: a Christian is someone who gives of himself.

We have to learn how to do this. This is why I am speaking to you. You need to learn how to give, not to give because you have to give, but because you want to give. I always tell people that I don't want their leftovers. Our poor don't need your pity. They don't need your sympathy. They need your love and compassion.

We need to have a life of prayer to be able to give like that. We need a life of sacrifice. Our Missionaries of Charity have consecrated their whole lives to the poorest of the poor. We have taken a special vow to offer whole-hearted, free service to the poorest of the poor. For us, Christ is hidden under the suffering appearance of anyone who is hungry, anyone who is naked, anyone who is homeless or dying.

Contemplatives of Christ

Christ will not deceive us. That is why our lives must be woven around the Eucharist. The Christ who gives of himself to us under the appearance of bread and the Christ who is hidden under the distressing disguise of the poor, is the same Jesus. Because of this, we missionaries are not simply social workers. A Christian cannot say, "I am a social worker." It isn't just doing a little social work. If we Christian men and women believe that we are feeding a hungry Christ and clothing a naked Christ, we are contemplatives from the very center of our homes, our lives, and our world. That is why I define our Missionaries of Charity as contemplatives in the heart of the world twenty-four hours a day.

Christ has not deceived us. He has made this a condition for our future life in heaven. "Come, blessed of my Father, for I was hungry, I was naked, homeless . . . , and you did it unto me."

To Understand the Poor
Is to Understand What Love Is

The poor are great people. The poor are wonderful people. I assure you that we receive more from them than they receive from us. I remember the days of the conflict in Bangladesh. We had ten million refugees in Calcutta and in the surrounding area. I asked the Indian government to allow a certain number of missionaries to come to our aid and work with us because we were overwhelmed. The government agreed and fifteen or sixteen congregations came to help us. Each of them said the same thing when they left India and Calcutta: we have received more than what we have given. We have been changed because we have lived with Christ. We understand now what it means to love and to be loved in return.

On one particular occasion when we were discussing food supplies and other such things, a senator from the United States said, "Turning our backs on the poor is the same as turning our backs on Christ." You can apply this truth to yourself. If you truly strive to give your whole lives to Christ and try to help people to see Christ in others, if you love Christ in your neighbor and love one another as Christ loves you, you will understand.

This is the only condition that Christ really places on us: "Love one another as I have loved you." And we know very well how much he has loved us! He died for us! He gave us his own mother before he died!

Jesus wants us to give of ourselves every moment. You have been taught by those who have given their whole lives to Christ.[3] By their teaching and personal example, they have kindled the light of Christ in your lives. The time has come for you to likewise kindle the same light of Christ in the lives of those around you.

A Lighted Lamp

We have a home in Australia where, as you know, many aborigines live in terrible conditions. When we first arrived there to help these people, we came upon an elderly man who lived in the worst of conditions. I went and tried to start up a conversation with him. I said to him, "Please let me clean your house and make up your bed." "I am fine like this," he replied. I said, "You will be better off with a clean house."

Finally he agreed. When I entered his house, which bore little resemblance to a home, I noticed a lamp. It was a beautiful lamp, but it was covered with filth and dust. I asked him, "Do you ever light that lamp?" He asked, "For whom? No one ever comes to my house. I spend days without ever seeing a human face. I have no need to light the lamp." Then I asked him if he would be willing to light the lamp if the sisters came to see him regularly. He answered, "Of course!"

The sisters made it their habit to visit him every evening. The old man began to light the lamp for them and to keep it clean. He began to keep his house clean, too. He lived for two more years.

Once he gave the sisters a message for me: "Tell my friend that the light that she lit in my life is still shining." It was a very small thing, but in that dark loneliness a light was lit and continued to shine.

This story will mean a lot to you who belong to Christ, to you who have received Jesus. You know what it means to be loved by Christ. You are aware of the divine commandment that we are to love one another as he has loved us.

Sharing Until It Hurts

Give! Give the love we have all received to those around you. Give until it hurts, because real love hurts. That is why you must love until it hurts.

You must love with your time, your hands, and your hearts. You need to share all that you have. Some time ago, we had great difficulty getting sugar in Calcutta. One day a small Hindu boy, not more than four years old, and his parents came and brought me a cup of sugar. The little boy said, "I did not eat sugar for three days. Give my sugar to your children." That little boy loved to the point of sacrificing.

On another occasion, a gentleman came to our house and said, "There is a Hindu family that has eight children. They haven't eaten anything for a long time." I instantly took some rice that we were going to use for supper and went with the gentleman to seek out that family. I could see the spectre of hunger drawn on the faces of the little children when we found the family. They looked like human skeletons. In spite of their need, the mother had the courage and compassion to divide the rice that I had brought into two portions. Then she went out.

When she came back I asked her, "Where did you go? What have you done?" She said, "They are hungry also."

"Who are they?" I asked. It seems a Moslem family with the same number of children lived across the street. She knew that they were hungry, too. What struck me was that she knew, and because she knew she gave until it hurt. That is something beautiful. That is love in action! That woman shared with great sacrifice.

I did not bring them more rice that night because I wanted them to experience the joy of loving and sharing. You should have seen the faces of those little children! They barely understood what their mother had done, yet their eyes shined with a smile. When I arrived again, they looked starved and sad. But what their mother did had taught them what real love is all about. This is how our poor are!

One night in Calcutta we picked up some people off the streets. One of them, a woman, was in desperate condition. I told the sisters that I would take care of her. So I did for her all that my love could do. When I put her in bed, she squeezed my hand tightly. A beautiful smile was on her face. I have never seen such a smile on another face. It was a very delicate smile. She didn't say more than two words, "Thank you." Then she died.

For a moment I asked myself, without taking my eyes off of her, what I would have said if I had been in her place? My answer was very simple. I would have tried to draw a little attention to myself. I would have said: "I am cold! I am dying!" Or I would have said something like that. That extraordinary woman gave me much more than what I gave her. She gave me her grateful love.

That is the way our people are. Do you know them? They may live in your own homes. There are lonely people everywhere. Do you realize that? Maybe they are at your side, right next to you. St. John the Evangelist has given us a clear understanding about this, "How can you say that you love God whom you do not see, if you do not love your neighbor whom you do see?" He defines what a person is who says he loves God but doesn't love his neighbor. He says that he is a liar!

Let us all pray, then. We all need to pray, to sacrifice, to be totally open to God. Then he can use us as he sees fit.

Hungry for God and Hungry for Love

People are hungry for God. People are hungry for love. Are you aware of that? Do you know that? Do you see that? Do you have eyes to see? Quite often we look but we don't see. We are all passing through this world. We need to open our eyes and see.

You have received a lot from your brethren: the gift of love. You have seen love in action through their lives. Take their example to heart, the example of sacrificial giving. Before anything else look for the poor in your own homes and on the street where you live. There are lonely people around you in hospitals and psychiatric wards. There are so many people that are homeless!

In New York, our sisters are working among the destitute who are dying. What pain it causes to see these people! They are only known by their street address now. Yet they were all someone's children. Someone loved them at one time. They loved others during their lifetime. But now they are only known by their street address.

The Poverty of Abortion

That is real poverty, but abortion causes a greater poverty. This is where your intervention is needed, too. You who have received so much love show your love by protecting the sacredness of life. That unborn child has been created in the image and likeness of God. God's life is present in that unborn child. There are those who destroy life because they are afraid that they will have to sacrifice to feed and educate one more child. They make that child die so that they can live more comfortably.

This is where you must sow love. The sacredness of life is one of the greatest gifts that God has given us. You who have received so much love share it with others. Love others the way that God has loved you, with tenderness. And pray for us.

Our sisters and brothers have surrendered their lives to the love of Christ, with an undivided love through chastity and the freedom of poverty. For us poverty is a necessity. We have to know what poverty is in order to be able to understand the poor. That is why we need the freedom to be poor with our total surrender through obedience.

If I belong to Christ, obedience is a way of being at his disposal so that he is free to use me as he wills. Our fourth vow that we profess is to give wholehearted, free service to the poorest of the poor, to Christ who is hidden under the distressing appearance of the poor.

At Jesus' Service

The first Christians died willingly for Jesus, and they were known for their love for one another. Never has the world had a greater need for love than in our day. People are hungry for love. We don't have time to stop and smile at each other. We are all in such a hurry! People are hungry for love. We have received so much!

Pray. Ask for the necessary grace. Pray to be able to understand how much Jesus loved us, so that you can love others. And pray for the sisters, that we won't spoil God's work. Pray that we allow Jesus to use each of us as he wishes and wherever he wishes.

We thank God because we have so many wonderful vocations. Young people come to us saying, "I am looking for a life of poverty, prayer, and sacrifice that will lead me to serve the poor." I am very grateful, especially to the people of Malta. Over the last two years groups of young people from Malta have come to Palermo to share in the sisters' work.[4]

There are other countries, too. But this one has been one of the most blessed by God. Be generous. Share what you have received with other countries like Yemen. For about eight hundred years that country was closed to all Christian contact. After all these years, our sisters have arrived, and people have become aware that God loves them. They have called the sisters "carriers of God's love." Why? Because they witness the sisters' desire to serve and to love. They realize that the sisters convert their love for Christ into deeds. That is why they say that this is the first time that they have seen Christian love expressed in concrete, living ways.

They find that God's mercy is shown through these sisters who are capable of doing what they undertake for the love of Christ, caring for the lepers, the dying, the crippled, and the unwanted. The Yemenites realize that these are women of God, messengers of his love on earth. Due to the sisters' presence in that land submerged in darkness, a light has been kindled in the lives of the Yemenites.

Pray that we don't spoil the work God has given us, and that it continues to be his work. Pray that you and I don't employ bombs and cannons to conquer the world. Let us use love and compassion to win the world, to bring the world the gospel of Christ. Let us all bring the good news that God loves the world!

TWO

My Vocation

My vocation is grounded in belonging to Jesus, and in the firm conviction that nothing will separate me from the love of Christ. The work we do is nothing more than a means of transforming our love for Christ into something concrete. I didn't have to find Jesus. Jesus found me and chose me. A strong vocation is based on being possessed by Christ. It means loving him with undivided attention and faithfulness through the freedom of poverty and total self-surrender through obedience. This is the call of being a Missionary of Charity, being wholeheartedly given over to serving the poorest of the poor. It means serving Christ through his suffering appearance in the poor:

He is the Life that I want to live.

Mother Teresa's comments on her vocation were recorded on tape in the streets of Rome, while she was visiting a slum. The recording was then translated into German and published in a booklet entitled "Der Weg und die Wahrheit und das Leben: Christus-Zeugnisse aus unserer Zeit" (*The Way, the Truth and the Life: Christian Testimonies in Our Time*). In spite of the distractions and the noise of the setting, Mother Teresa managed to share insights about her vocation and her deep love for Jesus, parts of which form a hymn of worship.

He is the Light that I want to radiate.
He is the Way to the Father.
He is the Love with which I want to love.
He is the Joy that I want to share.
He is the Peace that I want to sow.
Jesus is Everything to me.
Without him, I can do nothing.

Jesus is the Bread of Life that the church offers me. Only through him, in him, and with him can I live. He said, "If you do not eat my flesh and drink my blood, you will have no life within you." I know that he made himself the Bread of Life in order to satisfy my hunger for him and for his love. He, in turn, made himself the hungry one to satisfy my hunger for him through my love and service. He gives me the opportunity to feed him by feeding those who are hungry, to clothe him by clothing those who are naked, to heal him by caring for those who are sick, and to offer him shelter by housing those who are homeless and unwanted. This vision is what makes a Missionary of Charity a contemplative in the heart of the world.

Since we can touch Jesus in the poor, we can be in his presence twenty-four hours a day. He says, "And you did it unto me. I was hungry. I was naked. I was homeless . . . , and you did it unto me." Jesus in the Eucharist and Jesus in the poor, under the appearance of bread and under the appearance of the poor, makes us contemplatives in the heart of the world.

We are entirely at the disposal of the church. We profess a deep, personal love for the Holy Father. We surrender ourselves completely to be united with him as carriers of God's love. Pray for us that we don't spoil the work God has called us to. Let us pray together:

Make us worthy, Lord, to serve our brothers and sisters scattered throughout the entire world, who live and die in poverty and hunger. Through the service of our hands, give them their daily bread; and by our understanding love, give them peace and joy.

THREE

Holiness Is Everyone's Duty

Accepting the Poor

Let's thank God in prayer for giving us the opportunity to be together.[1] For my part, I thank God for giving me the chance to thank each and every one of you for the love and assistance that you have given and continue to give to our brothers.

I thank you for the love and trust with which you have welcomed them and the generous support you have given them. I also want to thank our poor, whom the brothers serve, for having accepted the brothers with so much love and kindness. We are greatly indebted to them because I don't think that the Missionary of Charity Brothers would be here if the poor had not welcomed them.

The talk was given by Mother Teresa to the Co-workers of the Missionary Brothers of Charity in Los Angeles, California on July 1, 1977. The Brothers have several missions in that city. Their address is: Missionaries of Charity, 1600 Ingraham St., Los Angeles, CA 90017.

But, above all, we are deeply grateful to Mother Church for allowing us to live our vocation, to be the presence of Jesus among the poorest of the poor. In that way, we are to be God's love and compassion for them.[2] God still loves the world. He continues loving it without fail. God so loved the world that he gave his only Son. God still loves the world and today he continues to give Jesus to the world through you and me. We must be like Jesus, God's gift, who came into the world because the Father loved the world. Each of us in his own way, must be the Father's love and compassion toward the world.

Sharing Jesus with Others

God gave his Son to Mary, the virgin immaculate. The very moment she said that she was the handmaid of the Lord and confessed her lowliness, saying that she was nothing, she was filled with grace. We know what happened afterwards. She began carrying Jesus in her womb, and she wanted to share him right away with others. She went as the servant of the Lord, even serving as his slave. She went in haste, as if there were not enough time, to share Jesus with others. We, too, must do the same. For her the day of the annunciation was her First Communion Day. Jesus came into her life, and she wanted to immediately share him with others. So should it be with us.

Jesus has become the Bread of Life so that we too, just like Mary, may carry him. We too, just like Mary, must be ready to go in haste to share the Jesus we bear with others. Like her, we must try to serve others with the presence of Christ.

The Hungry Christ

The reason why the vocation of the Missionary of Charity Brothers and Sisters and their co-workers is so beautiful is that it is a vocation for everyone. All of us have been given the opportunity to be completely possessed by Jesus. The work he has entrusted to you and me is nothing more than putting our love for him into action. What you do, I cannot do. What I do, you cannot do. But, together, you and I can do something beautiful for God.

That is why Jesus made himself the Bread of Life, to satisfy our hunger for God and for his love. I believe that was not enough for him. Jesus made himself the hungry one, the naked one, the destitute one who is dying. He said, "I was hungry, naked, sick, homeless . . . , and you did it to me." That is why I say that the Brothers and Sisters of Charity are not simply social workers. They are contemplatives in the heart of the world because they are in contact with the body of Christ twenty-four hours a day.

The truth applies to each of you also: in your homes and in every aspect of your lives. Jesus is still saying, "I was hungry." In your homes you have a starving Christ, a naked Christ, a homeless Christ. Are you capable of recognizing him in your own homes? Do you realize that he is right there in your midst?

How many times does a child run away from home because there is no one there to love him! How often it is that the elderly in the family are not at home. Instead, they are in nursing homes because no one has time for them.[3] The poor are right in your own homes. Are you aware of that?

Accepting and Giving

I remember some time ago when a group of teachers from the United States came to one of our houses. Before leaving, they asked me to tell them something that would be useful and would help them to be better people. I told them to smile at each other. We no longer have time to look at each other, much less to smile at one another. One of them asked me, "Are you married?" I said, "Yes, and sometimes I find it very difficult to smile at Jesus because he can be so demanding."

I believe we must look for holiness, joy, and love in our own homes. We must make our home like a second "Nazareth" where Jesus can come and live with us. Holiness is not a luxury, meant for only a few. It is a simple duty for each one of us. Holiness is to take whatever Jesus gives us and to give Jesus whatever he asks of us with a big smile. That is God's will. In your life, in mine, in the life of each of us, God has made us for bigger things. He has created us to love and to be loved, so that we walk toward our heavenly home. As we carry Jesus in the world, we will be prepared to return eagerly to our Father's house when the day arrives for us to be called home.

Loving Until It Hurts

Our poor are great people. They give us more than we give them. They can teach us so many beautiful things. They don't need our sympathy or our pity. They need our love and compassion. We don't have to love them from our abundance. We must love them until it hurts.

The same way Jesus allows himself to be broken and given to us as food, we, too, must divide and share what we have with others. First of all, we must share with those in our homes because love starts at home. From there, charity extends to our neighbors who are right next door, then to those who live on the same street, and from there to those in the city where we live.

To be true, love has to hurt. Our people, the poor, are great people because they give us a lot of love and joy by accepting us. They appreciate the little things we do for them.

Carriers of God's Love

Our brothers and sisters are found scattered around the world.[4] It is wonderful to see how people welcome us, to hear them exclaim, "The sisters and brothers are Christ's love among us." Remember me telling you how the sisters arrived in the Muslim country of Yemen. It was the first time in eight hundred years that a Catholic sister had been seen in that country. The head of the government of that country wrote to a priest in Rome, saying, "The sisters' presence has kindled a new light in the lives of our people." The sisters are not called Missionaries of Charity there. They are called the "Carriers of God's Love."[5]

In the same way, you and I must be carriers of God's love. Each time we receive Holy Communion we are filled with Jesus and we must, like our Lady, leave in haste and search out that run-away child and bring him home. We must bring him to where there is love, joy, peace—to the place where God is with us.

Pray for us that we won't spoil the work God has given us to do, so that we may move forward together with you, for this work has been entrusted to both you and us. All of us together must make something beautiful for God.

FOUR

A Call to Love

Our Lady's call was to accept Jesus into her life by responding to God, "Do unto me according to your word." She submitted to being the Lord's handmaid. She immediately went to share Jesus with St. John the Baptist and his mother. Today the same Jesus, the living Jesus transformed into the Bread of Life, still comes to us. When he comes to us we too, just like Mary, must go in haste to give him to others.

He became the Bread of Life to satisfy our hunger for God, but that was not enough for him. He became the hungry one, the naked one, and the homeless one. That way we, in turn, can satisfy his great love for us. He is still saying, "You did it to me." We can be with him twenty-four hours a day.

But what does this call mean to our young people

This address was given by Mother Teresa when she attended the Katholikentag, at the invitation of the German Catholic bishops in the Cathedral of Freiburg in Breisgau (September 16-17, 1978). The general theme of the event was "God's Call: Our Way" ("Gottes Anruf Unser Weg"). The German bishops also invited then Cardinal Karol Wojtyla, Archbishop of Cracow in Poland. But he was unable to attend due to the death of Pope Paul VI. The Conclave of Cardinals had been called to elect the next pope.

today? How can they respond? The answer is simple but profound.

Young people, with your lives you determine the outcome of his call to you. Will you accept it? It is a call to you and me. Every Christian soul is called to belong to God, some in a special way through the priesthood and the religious life.

Our vocation is to belong to Jesus so completely that nothing can separate us from the love of Christ. What you and I must do is nothing less than putting our love for Christ into practice. The important thing is not how much we accomplish, but how much love we put into our deeds every day. That is the measure of our love for God.

Our sisters and brothers are called Missionaries of Charity. Many of them are young people who heard the call to become carriers of God's love. For instance, the presence of the sisters has kindled a new light in the lives of many people in countries around the world. That is why the Muslim leader of a certain country wrote to Rome saying, "What are the sisters doing here? They are simply feeding the hungry Christ, clothing the naked Christ, and offering shelter to the homeless, unwanted Christ."

The amount of good works is not important. The key is the love that the sisters put into everything that they do. To be able to do this kind of work, not only for a day but for a lifetime, the sisters cleave to Jesus with an undivided love by means of their chastity, the freedom of poverty, and total submission to obedience. In our order, we profess a fourth vow to offer wholehearted, free service to the poorest of the poor. This vow—the vow of love—directs our attention completely to the poorest of the poor. It also pre-disposes us to depend totally upon God's providence.

Who are the poorest of the poor? They are the unwanted, the unloved, the ignored, the hungry, the naked, the homeless, the leper, and the alcoholic in our midst.

To live out such a calling every Missionary of Charity must have a life focused on the Eucharist. We see Christ in the Eucharist under the appearance of bread, while we see him in the poor under the distressing disguise of poverty. The Eucharist and the poor are nothing more than the same love of God. To be able to see and love Jesus in the poor, we must be one with Christ through a life of deep prayer. That is why the sisters start their day with Mass and medita-tion. And they finish it with adoration of the Blessed Sacrament. Communion with Christ gives us our strength, our joy, and our love.

The sisters care for forty-nine thousand lepers. They are among the most unwanted, unloved, and neglected people. The other day one of our sisters was washing a leper covered with sores. A Muslim holy man was present, standing close to her. He said, "All these years I have believed that Jesus Christ is a prophet. Today I believe that Jesus Christ is God since he has been able to give such joy to this sister, so that she can do her work with so much love."

In most cities where we have centers, we have homes for the destitute who are dying. We pick them up off the streets and bring them home. In Calcutta, alone, we have rescued thirty-six thousand people in twenty-five years. Seventeen thousand of them died while we were caring for them. They had beautiful deaths. One of them said, "I have lived like an animal in the streets. I am going to die like an angel, surrounded by love and care."

The poor are great people worthy of love. Do you know the poor in your country? Do you know the poor who live next door to you? Poverty is not only to be hungry for something to eat, to lack clothing, or not to have a home. Poverty is even greater when it is a poverty of the heart.

Our sisters work in many countries around the world. They work with society's outcasts. One day the sisters came across a man who had locked himself away from everyone. He lived in a tightly shut room. The sisters came in, washed his clothes, cleaned his room, and bathed him. All the while he did not say a word. Two days later he told the sisters: "You have brought God into my life. Bring me also a priest." The sisters brought him a priest, and he made his confession for the first time in sixty years. The next morning he died.

Oh, how great is the vocation of the priesthood! God had come into that man's life, but he needed a priest to come into contact with God's mercy and forgiveness. He needed the ministry of a priest to take away his sins, to wash his sins away in the precious blood of Christ.

You, young men, whom Jesus has called, whom Jesus has chosen for his own, consider the call to be that bridge that can link souls to God.

Let us not love by words alone, but let us love until it hurts. It cost Jesus to love us. He even died for us. Now it is our turn to love one another as Jesus loved us. You must not be afraid to say "yes" to Jesus, because there is no greater love than his love and no greater joy than his joy.

All of us must be saints in this world. Holiness is not a luxury for only a few. It is a duty for you and me. So let's be saints and give glory to the Father. That is why Jesus came to this earth. Being rich, he became poor out of love for us, so that we can be rich and fully share in the happiness of God for all eternity.

We have a mother in heaven, the Virgin Mary, who is a guide for us, a great joy, and an important source of our cheerfulness in Christ. Intercede with her before God. Pray the Rosary so that Mary may always be with you, to be your guide, to protect and keep you as a mother. Introduce prayer into your families. The family that prays together, stays together.

My prayer for you is that you come to understand and have the courage to answer Jesus' call to you with the simple word "yes." Also, pray for us that we will not spoil the work God has given us to do.

Now I would like to ask you to pray with me a prayer that the Missionaries of Charity say every day:

Make us worthy, Lord, to serve our brothers and sisters scattered throughout the entire world, who live and die in poverty and hunger. Through the service of our hands, give them their daily bread; and by our understanding love, give them peace and joy.
Lord, make me an instrument of your peace;
where there is hatred, let me sow love;
where there is injury, pardon;
where there is doubt, faith;
where there is despair, hope;
where there is darkness, light;
where there is sadness, joy.
O divine master, grant that I may not so much seek

to be consoled as to console;
to be understood as to understand;
to be loved as to love;
for it is in giving that we receive;
it is in pardoning that we are pardoned;
it is in dying that we are born to eternal life.
Amen.

FIVE

Children of God: Our Brothers and Sisters

God so loved the world that he gave his only begotten Son. Jesus said, "As the Father has loved me, so I have loved you." The Father's love, the Son's love, and our love is but a giving until it hurts. Christ has identified himself with the hungry, the sick, the naked. I mean the hungry who not only hunger for bread but for love and care. We need to want to be someone for someone who needs us. We need to be someone for the naked who not only lack clothing but mercy. We need to be someone for the destitute who not only lack a roof over their heads, but who are deprived of having someone who cares, someone to belong to.

The Crime of Abortion

Many of our children are unwanted and unloved.

This talk was given by Mother Teresa during a population and ecology conference in Sydney, Australia, on February 26, 1973.

They need someone to care. The problem that worries so many people today is not the fact that the world is beginning to be over-populated. What we are beginning to see more and more is that there are people who are trying to prove that God's providence cannot provide for all the children yet to be born. In my opinion, if abortion is allowed in the rich countries that have everything that money can buy, then those countries are the poorest among the poor.

In such countries, I would like to open homes for unwanted children, so I could welcome them and provide for each one of them. We have many such homes all over India. And we have never had to reject any child in need. The wonderful thing is that each child, who has been able to escape death at the hands of his or her own parents, has found a home with new parents.

Just last year in Calcutta, we started a campaign to prevent abortions through adoptions. And thanks be to God! We were able to give many children, who would have died otherwise, a father and a mother to love and care for them. For us in India, that is something wonderful, because those children are untouchables by law.[1] That is what is so wonderful about our people. They are willing to adopt and offer a home to these unwanted children, to surround these suffering images of Christ with affection.

As for countries that have passed laws that allow abortion—for those who consider it something natural and all right—we must pray for them. Their sin is great. It is a crime.

Adoption as an Alternative to Abortion

When we were invited to care for the young women of Bangladesh who had been raped by soldiers, we saw the need to open a home for them. We had to face many serious difficulties because sheltering women who had been raped went against both Muslim and Hindu laws. I repeat that we were faced with many serious difficulties. But once the Mujib (the prime minister) said that those young women were heroines of the nation— who had fought to save their purity and who had fought for their country—the girls' parents came to take care of them. In many cases, young men offered to marry them.

Then it occurred to some people to perform abortions on those women who had been raped and were found to be pregnant. So we had to wage a tremendous struggle against those who favored abortion. I told these people that our young women had been violated, that they had been forced against their will, that they did not want to sin. "Whereas, what you are trying to force them to commit is a transgression that they will remember for the rest of their lives," I said. "They will never forget that they were mothers who killed their own children."

Thanks be to God! The government accepted our proposal. The women were told that each child who was to be aborted should be taken to the house of Mother Teresa. There they would receive care. And of the forty children that we have received, more than thirty have been adopted by wonderful families in

Canada and other countries. This is a concrete example of how we have prevented abortions through adoptions.

Natural Family Planning

Since our sisters work in the slums of forty cities all over India, we have found among our poor many instances of young mothers who were dying and many children with deformities or defects. At first, we couldn't find the cause. Investigating further we discovered that these women were the victims of their own ignorance. We decided to ask God to send us someone who could take on the work of helping such women, someone who could help them cope with their problem with a clear conscience and a healthy body. Then they could make a happy home for themselves and for their children.

God answered our prayers. He sent us a young woman from Mauritius Island who had experience in helping married couples practice natural family planning in her own country. We started up our information program. Today there are more than three thousand families that use natural family planning and it has been about 95 percent effective.

As soon as her work became well established in India, we gave that sister the responsibility of training novices in the method of natural family planning. Then we sent them out into the slums. Now the Indian government has sent a group of highly qualified men to investigate natural family planning. They have heard of our work in this area and have verified that other methods of family planning run great risks to our poor. I ask you to pray that they will find the results they are looking for. Then, if it be God's will, may they effectively interpret what they have discovered about natural family planning and apply it at the national level.

When our people in India saw the good effects of this approach to family planning in their own families, they came to thank me for allowing the sisters to carry out this work among them. Some told us: "Our family is healthy. Our family is united. And we can have a baby whenever we want." Because of this, there is now more unity at home. There is more love and mutual respect among spouses. Also, there is more joy. Economic hardships have been lessened by using this method.

We want to show our people that God loves them and that they are more important to him than the lilies of the field and the sparrows. God loves them and provides for them.

Our Brothers and Sisters

If our poor have at times starved to death, it is not because God doesn't care for them. Rather, it is because you and I have refused to give food to them. We have not been instruments of love in God's hands, so that he can give them bread or offer them clothing. It has happened because, once again, we have not recognized Christ under the disguise of suffering in the hungry. We have not recognized him in the one who suffers from loneliness. We have not recognized him in the homeless child looking for shelter.

Some time ago a small child came to our door around midnight. I went down and opened the door for him. The child was crying and he said to me, "I went to my mother and she didn't want me. I went to my father and he wouldn't accept me either. Please love me. You, at least." That is a situation that is repeated every day in many places.

You also have people who are unloved and unwanted. Yet they are, just like us, children of God. Even more, they are Christ in our midst and they belong to us. They are our brothers and sisters.

The same hunger exists in India and in Europe, for example. It exists wherever the sisters find Christ under the appearance of suffering. It is possible that in Australia, in Europe, and in the United States, it isn't always hunger for a piece of bread or a garment of clothing. Everywhere there exists that same loneliness, the same deep need to be loved and cared for. Right in your midst there are those who suffer because they do not feel wanted or loved. They experience the anguish of having no one to call their own. This is real poverty without a doubt.

We must believe Christ who does not deceive us and who says, "I was hungry and you gave me to eat. I was naked and you clothed me. I was homeless and you offered me shelter. As often as you did it to the least of my brethren, you did it to me!"

We have picked up more than thirty-six thousand people off the streets of Calcutta. We pick them up and take them to our home for the poor who are dying. They die so peacefully. They die serenely in God's presence. The sisters can testify to this. We have never found a single man or woman who has refused to say to God, "I repent." We have not found one who has refused to say to God, "My God, I love you."

Love One Another

We have thousands of lepers. They are so great, so beautiful inside in spite of their physical disfigurement. Last Christmas I was with them. There are thousands of our lepers, and we always hold a Christmas party for them. I told them at the party that they are a gift from God. God has a special love for them. He accepts them. What they have is not a sin. That is what I told them.

An elderly man, completely disfigured by leprosy, tried to get close to me. He said to me, "Say it again. That has been good for me. I have always heard that no one loves us. It is wonderful to know that God loves us. Say it again."

In Melbourne, Australia, we have a home of compassion. We have people who have no one. We have those who roam the streets, for whom maybe jail and the road are the only places to call home. One of them had been badly hurt by a friend of his, who was also a resident at our home. Thinking that the matter was very serious, someone asked that man who had been hurt, "Who did that to you?" He would not reveal the name of the one who had hurt him. After the person had gone away, I asked him, "Why didn't you tell who hurt you?" The man looked at me and said, "His suffering is not going to lessen my suffering." This is what Jesus meant when he said, "Love one another as I have loved you."

SIX

God Loves Us

Mary, the First Missionary of Charity

Let's give thanks to God for bringing us together, we who belong to him in a special way. He has created us for greater things: to love and to be loved; to be holy as he is holy. God so loved the world that he gave his only Son Jesus to the immaculate Virgin Mary. The very first Holy Communion was celebrated at the very moment Jesus came into her life. Immediately, she left in haste to share Jesus with others. Mary was, in a way, the first Missionary of Charity—the first carrier of God's love.

From then until now, you and I have not stopped receiving that same Jesus. We, like Mary, have the privilege of taking him to others. Jesus loved us, and he still loves us. He loved and still loves the lepers, the destitute who are dying, the alcoholics, the unwanted, and the unloved. He loves them deeply. He died for them, and he doesn't stop saying: "Love one another as I have loved you. As the Father loves me, love one

---

This address was given by Mother Teresa in Dublin, Ireland, on June 2, 1979. Approximately five thousand persons gathered at a Carmelite church to hear the address.

another. I have loved you as my Father loves me."

The Father loved Jesus and gave him to us. Jesus made himself the Bread of Life, so that we could eat of him and have life. He wants to satisfy our hunger for love and for God.

Under the Disguise of the Poor

As if that were not enough, Jesus became the hungry one, so that you and I could satisfy his hunger, cover his nakedness, and offer him shelter. He said, "You did it to me. I was hungry. I was naked. I was homeless." The forgotten man in the street, the one we picked up in the streets of Calcutta, was Jesus bearing that man's appearance. It was Jesus who was hungry. I will never forget the man who was half-eaten by worms when we found him. He was tenderly carried to the home for dying destitutes. On the way, he murmured: "I have lived like an animal, but now I am going to die loved and surrounded with care." That is how he died and went home to God. That was Jesus under the disguise of the poor.

One of our novices had come from a far-off country[1] and a well-to-do family. She was sent right away to our home for the destitute who are dying, just like the rest of the novices. Before they left I told them, "During Mass you have seen with what care and tenderness the priest touched the body of Christ changed into the Bread of Life. Do the same in the home for dying destitutes."

Three hours later the novices returned. The newly arrived novice came up to me and said full of joy, "Mother, I have been touching the body of Christ for three hours!" I asked her, "What have you done?" She said that she had rescued a man lying in the gutter, half-eaten by worms. "I really felt that I was touching the body of Christ as Jesus said, 'I was sick . . . ,'" she continued.

That young sister was a contemplative. She had been touching Christ for three hours and offering her love to him. To be able to do the same, it is necessary to know the poor.

The poor are great people. The poor deserve love. Do you know the poor in your midst? It would be sad if you didn't know your own poor. Just as love begins at home, so too poverty begins at home. You need to know who is lonely, unloved, and forgotten in your own homes.

Loving Children

An incredible poverty exists today. Unborn children are aborted because they are unwanted. Children die in their mother's wombs because they are unwanted. A nation that allows abortion is a very poor one. A mother who is capable of killing her own child only because she is afraid of having another one is poor indeed! She is afraid of feeding one more child and educating one more child. She prefers to have another television set or an automobile instead. A child condemned to death for that! Nevertheless, we read in Scripture: "Even if a mother should forsake her child, I will not forsake you. I have you in the palm of my hand."

If a mother can kill her own child, how long will it be before we start to kill one another? We should not be surprised when we hear about murders, deaths, wars, and hate in the world today. Don't ever allow even one child, born or unborn to be unwanted. Let's go with our Lady to search out that child and take him or her home.

Sharing with the Poor

There is in the world today a great hunger for God. Everywhere there is so much sin caused by broken homes! Fathers and mothers don't have the time to pray together. If the family doesn't pray together, if the children aren't united with their parents in prayer, how are they going to stay together? Nazareth was truly Nazareth because Jesus, Mary, and Joseph stayed together. They stayed together precisely because they prayed together. If we really want peace, we don't need to resort to weapons and bombs. Let's bring prayer into our lives and into our homes. Let's bring love and peace into our homes, and we will begin to experience peace on earth.

Love, to be real, must hurt. If you want to truly love the poor, you must share with them. If you want poverty to disappear, share it. A gentleman asked me, "What must we do to eliminate poverty from India?" I answered, "We need to learn to share with the poor."[2]

That is what I want to share with you. We cannot share unless our lives are full of God's love and our hearts are pure. As Jesus said, "Blessed are the pure of heart, for they shall see God." Unless we are able to see God in our neighbor, it will be very hard for us to love. Since love begins at home, let's love each other at home. Jesus said, "Love one another as I have loved you." He loved until it hurt. Jesus' love is so overwhelming that you and I can love him and find life. We can love Jesus in the hungry, the naked, and the destitute who are dying. We can love him because our prayer gives us the faith we need to be able to love. If you love, you will be willing to serve. And you will find Jesus in the distressing disguise of the poor.

Understanding the Poor

As you well know, our sisters and brothers live totally committed to the poorest of the poor. We need the vow of poverty because we must understand the poor. In order to understand the poor, we have to know what poverty is. We need to be poor. That is why in our congregation poverty is freedom for us. May it also be our strength and our joy!

We belong to Jesus. Our vocations belong to him. We are not there for the work but to belong to Jesus. Our work with the poor is nothing more than our love for God put into practice. In your family, if it is your vocation to have a family, love one another as husband and wife and have a family. The service you perform and the work you accomplish are your love for God put into practice.

In our congregation, we profess a fourth vow to offer wholehearted, free service to the poorest of the poor. Our service is totally free of charge and we depend completely upon God's providence. We take God at his word. Jesus said, "You are more important to my Father than the lilies of the field and the birds of the air." And we can truly testify to this truth. There has never been a day in which we have had to refuse somebody or have had no food or have been short a bed or something of the sort. And this is true in spite of the fact that we deal with thousands of people. We now have fifty-three thousand lepers alone. But not one of them has ever been rejected due to a lack of resources. God continually provides even though we do not have salaries, income, or anything of that sort. We receive freely, and we give freely. This has been such a beautiful gift from God.

We have witnessed God's tender care for us in a thousand ways. In Calcutta alone we care for seven thousand people daily. If one day we don't cook, they don't eat. One Friday morning the sister in charge of the kitchen came to me and said, "Mother, there is no food for Friday and Saturday. We should tell the people that we will have nothing to give them today or tomorrow." I was shocked. I didn't know what to tell her. But around nine o'clock in the morning, the Indian government for some unknown reason closed the public schools. Then all the bread for the school-children was sent to us. Our children, as well as all our seven thousand needy ones, ate bread and even more bread for two days. They had never eaten so much bread in their lives. No one in all of Calcutta could find out why the schools had been closed. But I knew. I knew it was God's tender care. I knew it was his tender loving care.

Believing in Love

Let's believe in God's love, and let's be faithful to him. If you look at the cross, you will see his head lowered to kiss you. You will see his arms stretched out to embrace you. You will see his heart open to welcome you. Don't be afraid. He loves us, and he wants us to love one another. He loves us in spite of how poor and sinful we are. His love is true, and we should believe in his love. If we truly believe, it will not be hard for us to identify with the poor, even the poor in our own homes.

Hungry for Love

Some weeks ago,[3] our sisters went out at night. Sometimes they work at night picking up abandoned people in the streets. Late that night they came across a young man alone in the street. They said to him, "You shouldn't be here. You should be with your parents."

He replied, "When I go home, my mother doesn't want me because I have long hair. Everytime I go back, she kicks me out of the house."

Later when the sisters came back that way, they found that the same young man had taken an overdose of something. They had to take him to the hospital. I could not help but think that very possibly his mother was concerned about the hunger of our people in India, but here was her own son who was hungry for love and care. Yet she had rejected him.

Bring love into your homes. If you truly love God, start loving your son or your daughter and your spouse. And the elderly, where are they? In nursing homes! Why are they not with you? And where is the retarded child? In an institution! Why is he not with you? That child, young mothers and fathers, is a gift from God.

The Irish people have been known for their belief in the sacredness of family life. Don't ever allow that belief to die out. It is a gift from God. The Irish people have been known for their faithfulness to the Rosary, to community prayer. Don't allow that faithfulness to vanish. It is a gift that God has given us all. The Irish people have taken the Word of God to many mission fields by giving up their sons to that vocation. That is God's gift to you and your families. Such beautiful vocations are God's gift. Don't be unfaithful now. The Irish have taken the Word of God to so many countries through their sons. Let's not ever stop nurturing the life of Christ in those countries.

We need your sons as priests and missionaries. We need to bring God into their lives so they can serve him. Ask God to grant that gift to your families. Bring prayer back into your lives. Defend the sacredness of the family. By doing so, you will be able to give up your sons and daughters to God with deep joy. The family that prays together, stays together. A family that sacrifices together and suffers together, shares in Christ's passion.

My prayer for you is a prayer of thanksgiving for this call Christ has given you. Fifty years ago I myself came from Yugoslavia to enter the Order of the Sisters of Our Lady of Loreto (known as the "Irish Ladies") in Rathfarnham[4] before leaving for India. That is my small connection with the Irish people and their missionary spirit. But perhaps it isn't so small, because in Ireland I learned to love God and to serve him faithfully. My sincere gratitude to the people of Ireland springs from that and for all that they have done for our mission countries, for their sons who have sown the Word of God.

The main intention of my prayer is that God may help all of us to remain faithful to the great gift that we have received. We must continue to make sacrifices. May God bless you and give you his grace.

At the same time, pray for us that we will not spoil the work God has given us to do. Pray that this wonderful call to reach the poorest of the poor may continue to be his work. Pray that no other desire or interest may interfere and spoil it. Pray that we may be faithful to Christ in the Eucharist, under the appearance of bread; and pray that we may be faithful to him under the distressing appearance of the poor.

SEVEN

Giving Is Sharing

Finding Jesus in the Poor

To be a co-worker is a gift from God. It is not simply a title. It means to be an active co-worker with Christ. The name of "Mother Teresa" is frequently referred to in our work, but really you and I are co-workers with Christ. That is why I say that being a co-worker is a gift from God. It is a hidden grace. We don't see it, but it is really a gift from God. Why has God chosen you? Why me? This is a mystery.

To be able to do something beautiful for God, we need Jesus. Jesus became the Bread of Life so that you and I, and even a small child, can receive him and have life. In a special way we need the Bread of Life to know the poor, to love them, and serve them. Each one of us needs to encounter Jesus. Without him, we can do nothing. We need the Bread of Life to live. Jesus said very clearly, "If you do not eat my flesh and drink my blood, you will not have eternal life."

This talk was given by Mother Teresa at Brompton Oratory in London on June 13, 1977 to the Co-workers of the Missionaries of Charity in England. On that occasion Joan Osborne succeeded Margaret Merryweather as national chairman of the co-workers.

This is the most wonderful surprise for all of us. To satisfy our love for God, Jesus made himself the Bread of Life. Let's marvel at God's hunger for us. He makes himself the hungry one, the naked one, the dying one. In that way he gives us the opportunity to feed him, to clothe him, and to aid him through our service to the poorest of the poor.

Here a beautiful standard for judgment presents itself. We have to become increasingly aware that the poor are the hope of humanity, for we will be judged by how we have treated the poor. We will have to face this reality when we are summoned before the throne of God: "I was hungry. I was naked. I was homeless. And whatever you did to the least of my brethren, you did it to me."

Recall that momentous event in St. Paul's life when he was touched by Jesus on the way to Damascus. Jesus asked him "Saul, Saul, why do you persecute me? I am Jesus whom you are persecuting." Jesus did not say, "I am the people of Damascus," or even "I am the Christian people." He said, "I am Jesus." In the same way, we have seen many times in the history of the church where Jesus has personally identified himself with the poor. He has shown a very personal concern for how they are treated.

For this very reason, I always tell Christians, as well as non-Christians, that we are not merely social workers. No co-worker or Missionary of Charity is a social worker. If we take Jesus at his word, all of us are contemplatives in the heart of the world, for if we have faith, we are continually in his presence. We need a life of prayer to have this kind of faith. We need to worship God and have a spirit of sacrifice. We need to spiritually feed ourselves on him constantly.

In the beginnings of our congregation, we used to have adoration of the Blessed Sacrament once a week. At our last general meeting[1] or convocation, there was a unanimous concensus on the part of all the sisters that there should be daily adoration. We now have an hour of adoration before the Blessed Sacrament every day. Upon returning home, we spend an hour alone worshiping Jesus in the Blessed Sacrament. I believe that this has been the greatest gift to our congregation. It is something that has worked important changes in our lives. It has brought us closer together and made us more understanding. It has helped us to know our poor better. It has fostered a greater tenderness and love in us. We owe it all to Jesus in the Blessed Sacrament. We cannot be co-workers or Missionaries of Charity without an intense life of prayer.

Young People Don't Want Compromises

The generosity of our young people is surprising. In Calcutta alone, we have 267 novices at this time.[2] You can just imagine our mother house with everything up in the air. Our many novices have to sleep in every available spot. There isn't a square foot of unused space in the mother house. This situation often reminds me of the Holy Family when "there was no room for them in the inn." The novices even have to sleep on top of our tables, on the floor, and on our benches. I can assure you that there isn't any empty space. If we try to put in one more bed, we find that there is no space for it. But I am not saying this to complain.

In Rome alone, we have forty-nine novices representing eighteen different nationalities.[3] The English, Irish, Spanish, and French nationalities are represented among them. God is drawing young people to us from all over the world.

There is something wonderful about the idealism and level of commitment among young people. We hand them a sheet of paper on which to answer this question: why do I want to become a Missionary of Charity? They all answer in more or less this way: "I am looking for a life of poverty, prayer, and sacrifice that will lead me to serve the poor." We often think that young people are attracted to a life of action. It may surprise you to know that what really attracts them is a life of poverty. They want only one thing: it is all or nothing with no compromises.

I want to give you a beautiful example of this. A very rich young woman wrote to me. She said, "Jesus has been inviting me to become a religious sister for several years. I have tried to find out where Jesus wants me to go. I have seen that in some places the sisters have the same things that I have, so I would not have to give up anything."

As you can see, here is a young woman who wants to give up everything so she can be free. Poverty is freedom for us. We all want to be rich in some measure. I can tell you this: if I could have only one sari, it would be *mine*. Yet if I become a Missionary of Charity, I am given a sari to *use*, not to keep. This is the difference between having your own sari and receiving one to use. That difference has been our strength and our joy.

Poverty and Freedom

Poverty is joy for us. Poverty is freedom for us. Poverty is an offering that we make to God. It is something that brings us very close to Jesus. I don't mean that poverty consists of simply not having things. We don't become rich by having money, property, or possessions. That isn't the question.

What is poverty? Poverty is freedom. It is a freedom so that what I possess doesn't own me, so that what I possess doesn't hold me down, so that my possessions don't keep me from sharing or giving of myself. This is the reason why many times I have told nuns, and even priests, who are in charge of educating the children of the wealthy: don't make the mistake of serving the riches of those children instead of the children for whom Jesus died. You must offer your love to him. Whatever you do at your school or at your university, you can do it for Jesus, just as we do it for Jesus in the slums of the poorest of the poor.

Jesus must be brought to every man and woman. Jesus is the only answer. You, as co-workers, must be free yourselves. If you use the name "Mother Teresa" in your work, that is only because it is a means to serving and loving Christ in the poor. In the bottom of your heart, you must be convinced that you and I are together co-workers of Christ. As such, you must be very close to him. You must share with him. You must be at his complete disposal.

The last time we had a meeting of co-worker coordinators in the United States, I told them, "Every co-worker must be at Christ's disposal to such a degree that Christ can make use of him without having to ask, May I? Can't I? Will you allow me? In other words, without previous consent. It is something very beautiful and freeing to be able to give ourselves fully to Jesus, each of us in our own way, each one of us in our own family."

I always say—and I don't get tired of repeating it—that love starts at home. I will never forget that I was in a country once where there were many coworkers, but two of the coordinators for the coworkers were very distant from each other. And they were husband and wife. They came to me and I told them, "I can't understand how you are able to give Jesus to others if you can't give him to each other. How can you find Jesus hidden under the distressing appearance of the poor if you cannot see him in each other?"

The husband and wife started up an endless argument. Both of them let out all their frustrations and hurts, saying everything they had to say. Then I interrupted. "Now that's enough. You have said everything that you needed to say. Let's go to Jesus so that you can tell him all these things."

We went to the chapel and the two knelt down before the altar. After a few moments, the husband turned to his wife and said, "You are my only love in this world, the only one I love and have." Other things of that sort followed. It was all very beautiful.

Now all the co-workers there have changed for the better. Why? Because those in charge of the group have come to understand that if we don't accept Jesus in one another, we will not be able to give him to others.

The very same thing happens in our congregation. All our homes should be little "Nazareths" where Jesus can come to rest for a while in our company, for the work we do is only a means and not an end in itself. No matter how beautiful the work may be, it is still just a simple means. After all, what matters is to belong to Jesus. The work we do is our love for Christ transformed into deeds. It is the same for you and for each one of your co-workers.

I believe that we have at the present time more than eighty thousand co-workers throughout the world.[4] Each one of them has to face the fact that as co-workers they belong to Christ. When I speak to non-Christians, I tell them that they belong to God, and they understand me. They understand that we all belong to the one from whose hand we have all come. It is for this reason that we must be capable of letting him live through our lives.

Seeing the Good in Others

There are little things that inevitably happen in our lives and in our homes. Misunderstandings and suffering come to everyone, even in our own congregation. Someone said to me one day, "You never talk to us about problems." I said that I didn't need to talk about such things precisely because everyone knows that there are always problems. What I do have to say again and again is that sometimes it seems we aren't aware of them when we should be. We don't recognize that a problem exists. This is something that often happens. Let's focus more on the things we ought to do in serving our husband, our wife, our children, our brothers—rather than on other people's shortcomings.

One year I wanted to do something special for our sisters. I sent out a newsletter to each one of them, to each community, suggesting that each one write down what she thought was beautiful in her sisters and in her community. I asked that each sister send her answer to me. Just imagine! A thousand letters arrived. I had to sit down and patiently read each one, making a list of each community and all the sisters. Later I returned the letters to the communities.

The sisters were surprised that someone would notice such beautiful things in them—that there was someone who was able to see them. All of this fostered a beautiful spirit of love, understanding, and sharing.

I feel that we too often focus only on the negative aspect of life, on what is bad. If we were more willing to see the good and the beautiful things that surround us, we would be able to transform our families. From there, we would change our next-door neighbors and then others who live in our neighborhood or city. We would be able to bring peace and love to our world which hungers so much for these things.

I have another conviction that I want to share with you. Love begins at home, and every co-worker should try to make sure that deep family love abides in his or her home. Only when love abides at home can we share it with our next-door neighbor. Then it will show forth and you will be able to say to them, "Yes, love is here."

And then you will be able to share it with everyone around you.

We don't need guns or bombs to bring peace to the world. We must share the peace that is in our own homes. I believe—and each of you is certainly aware of it—that every day we seem to have less and less time for sharing. There is even less time in our busy day to share a smile with those in our own families. There is no one at home to hug the children. Everyone is so busy! And the elderly are in nursing homes. There is no one at home to play with the children, to spend time with them. That's why so many children end up on the streets.

I think that our co-workers should consider it their duty to seek out those children and bring them home. In the United States, we started up a group of young people—even though they are not officially co-workers—who have heard the call to seek out these children, just like Mary, who went searching for the boy Jesus to bring him home after he had gotten lost and stayed in the temple. We must go find these children and bring them home; for if the children return, the parents will be affected, also.

A certain priest I knew was right when he used to say, "The family that prays together, stays together." Our prayer also has this purpose. We need to be able to pray. We need prayer just like we need air. Without prayer, we can do nothing. Someone asked me a few days ago what advice I had for politicians. I don't like to get involved in politics, but my answer just popped out, "They should spend time on their knees. I think that would help them to become better statesmen."

This is what we need to do when we go to share with others. For example, every time we need to make a decision concerning our families, we need to pray. Jesus said, "Ask and you will receive. Seek and you will find. Knock and the door will be opened." Nothing will be denied you. Our congregation is living proof of that. We are now more than a thousand.[5] Thousands of lives depend on us. In spite of that, we have never, never, never had to say to anybody, "Go away. We can't do anything for you." God is always there showing us that he never leaves our prayers unanswered. And to confirm this, since we are more important than the lilies of the field, God always helps us.

Working and Praying

There is only one little detail to add: we must join our prayer with work. We try to bring this across to our sisters by inviting them to make their work a prayer. How is it possible to change one's work into a prayer? Work cannot substitute for prayer. Nevertheless, we can learn to make work a prayer. How can we do this? By doing our work with Jesus and for Jesus. That is the way to make our work a prayer. It is possible that I may not be able to keep my attention fully on God while I work, but God doesn't demand that I do so. Yet I can fully desire and intend that my work be done with Jesus and for Jesus. This is beautiful and that is what God wants. He wants our will and our desire to be for him, for our family, for our children, for our brethren, and for the poor.

The poor are a gift that God bestows on us. But they need our life of prayer and our oneness with God. Real prayer is union with God, a union as vital as that of the vine and the branches, which is the illustration Jesus gives us in the Gospel of John. We need prayer. We need that union to produce good fruit. The fruit is what we produce with our hands, whether it be food, clothing, money, or something else. All of that is the fruit of our oneness with God. We need a life of prayer, of poverty, and of sacrifice to do this with love.

Sacrifice and prayer complement each other. There is no prayer without sacrifice, and there is no sacrifice without prayer. They complement each other. That is what Jesus has shown us. Jesus' life was spent in intimate union with his Father as he passed through this world doing good. We need to do the same. A co-worker is a co-worker of Christ. Let's walk by his side. We need to give Christ a chance to make use of us to be his word and his work—to share his food and his clothing in the world today. We must be capable of seeing Christ in the world. If we do not radiate the light of Christ around us, the sense of the darkness that prevails in the world will increase. The people around us should be able to recognize him by our union with God.

This is one of the things that most impresses me. Wherever I go, I always hear about co-workers who love one another in such a way that no one is able to sow disunity in their midst. There is a oneness of spirit and soul that binds them together, so that their oneness is unaffected even if they are sometimes far away from each other. This harmony is something that you must guard carefully. Don't let anything come between you and your co-worker or threaten your harmony. If such a thing should happen, you will be co-workers in name only and not from the heart.

We must love with Jesus' love and his spirit of sacrifice. God loved us by giving himself to us. Mary loved us by sharing Jesus with us. Jesus loved us by giving up his life for us and giving his body to us as the Bread of Life. We too must give ourselves to one another. Because of this, we must reject whatever would keep us from giving ourselves to one another. We must look at it as something dangerous, something that would destroy us. I think that anything that destroys or opposes this unity cannot come from God. It comes from the devil. Just as St. Ignatius says, whatever perverts or destroys comes from the devil. The devil is the father of lies. He is capable of telling us a whole pack of lies in hopes of destroying us.

Money Is a Means, Not an End in Itself

The last time we had a meeting of co-workers in Germany,[6] I insisted that we should increasingly deepen our life of love, humility, and sharing among all co-workers. At that time I said that I did not want our co-workers to become a group of mere fundraisers. I think I was misunderstood. I didn't mean to say that there is no need for money, since the truth is quite the contrary. I recall, for example, that for the past ten to fifteen years schoolchildren in India have been sending bread to our children in the slums. And English children have been sending milk, while German children have been sending vitamins. The result of all this love in action has been the prevention of epidemics among children in the slums. Thanks to the generosity of other children, we have not had cases of tuberculosis among our children. As you can see, it is not true that we don't need money.

All in all, I don't know how the word has spread that Mother Teresa doesn't need money, which is contrary to the facts since we depend totally on God's providence. What I meant to say at that occasion—even though I didn't manage to say it clearly enough—was that we must not make fundraising an end in itself.[7] I meant to say that we are not going to work like dogs day and night to raise funds, or try to raise more funds than this or that country. That is simply not our way. But it was not my intent, or the intent of my interpreter, to say that we will refuse gifts of money or that people should stop sending it to us. The aid and assistance of our co-workers should not be cut back either.

In any case, let it be clear that money is not an end but a means. Without money, for example, it would be impossible for us to feed more than seven thousand people daily in Calcutta. We spend around 20,000 rupies (equivalent to 1,600 U.S. dollars) a week just on food for the fifty-nine centers that we have in Calcutta, including homes for the poor who are dying, abandoned children, the elderly, and lepers. The money comes from sacrifices that people have made.

Giving Is Sharing

I don't want people donating just to get rid of something. There are people in Calcutta who have so much money that they want to get rid of it. The government puts pressure on the wealthy. They sometimes have money to spare, money that they try to hide.

In some cases they make a package, write the name of Mother Teresa on it, and then send it.

A few days ago I received a package wrapped in plain paper. I thought that it might contain stamps, cards, or something like that, so I put it aside. I planned to open it later when I had the time. A few hours later I opened it without even suspecting its contents. It was hard for me to believe my eyes. That package contained 20,000 rupies. It didn't have a return address or any note, which made me think that it might be money owed to the government.

I don't like people to send me something because they want to get rid of it. Giving is something different. It is sharing.

Not so long ago a very wealthy Hindu lady came to see me. She sat down and told me, "I would like to share in your work." In India, more and more people like her are offering to help. I said, "That is fine." The poor woman had a weakness that she confessed to me. "I love elegant saris." Indeed, she had on a very expensive sari that probably cost around 800 rupies. Mine cost only eight rupies. Hers cost one hundred times more. Then I asked the Virgin Mary to help me give an adequate answer to her question of how she could share in our work. It occurred to me to say to her, "I would start with the saries. The next time you go buy one, instead of paying 800 rupies, buy one that costs five hundred. Then with the extra 300 rupies, buy saris for the poor."

The good woman now wears 100-rupie saris, and that is because I have asked her not to buy cheaper ones. She has confessed to me that this has changed her life. She now knows what it means to share. That woman assures me that she has received more than what she has given. That is the way it is with our co-workers.

For that to be so, we need prayer. We need to pray together. We need to bring prayer into our family life. Through prayer, we will be able to teach our children and relatives to share. We will get more through genuine prayer than with mere words. We should not use words alone to convince people to give us money. Prayer and our words of request must go together. We can't do one without the other. They have to complement each other.

First, the Needs of the Body

We need money, medicines, clothing, and a thousand other things for the poor we serve. If so many people weren't generous, thousands would be left unaided. Because we still have many poor, needy children and families that live in the streets—not only in Calcutta but in London, Rotterdam, Madrid, Marseille, and Rome—the need is great. In the last city I mentioned, we have many needy. The sisters go out at night into the streets, especially around the train station, between 10 P.M. and 2 A.M. to pick up the homeless and take them to the home we have on San Gregorio al Celio.[8]

The last time that I was in Rome, I found it unbearable to see so many homeless people living that way. So I went to see the mayor of Rome and said, "Give me a place for these people, because they refuse to come with us and would rather stay where they are." The man who listened to me was a communist.

Everyone knows that the mayor of Rome is a communist.[9] He and his staff responded wonderfully. In a few days they offered us a very nice place near the Termini Train Station. At present, all those who have nowhere else to spend the night, except in the streets, go there and sleep in beds. In the morning they leave.

It is a beautiful work that is being shared by many people. It has come about through many meetings, through sharing the same thoughts and accepting some sacrifices. Prayer and sacrifice are always necessary. Our strength to accomplish our work always comes from prayer and sacrifice.

I don't think there is anyone who needs God's help and grace as much as I do. Sometimes I feel so helpless and weak. I think that is why God uses me. Because I cannot depend on my own strength, I rely on him twenty-four hours a day. If the day had even more hours, then I would need his help and grace during those hours as well. All of us must cling to God through prayer and sacrifice. Only then will we be able to see Christ in the needs of our neighbor.

The Gospels remind us that Jesus, before he taught the people, felt compassion for the multitudes that followed after him. Sometimes he felt it even to the point of forgetting to eat. How did he put his compassion into practice? He multiplied the loaves of bread and the fish to satisfy their hunger. He gave them food to eat until they couldn't eat any more, and twelve basketfuls were left over. Then he taught them. Only then did he tell them the good news. This is what we must often do in our work: we must first satisfy the needs of the body, so we can then bring Christ to the poor.

An Atheist Becomes a Believer

To bring Christ to others depends on how we do what we do for the poor. We could do it one way, or we could do it in some other way. I will never forget the time when a certain man visited our home for the poor who are dying. He arrived just as the sisters were bringing in some of the dying off the streets. They had picked a man out of the gutter, and he was covered with worms. Without knowing she was being watched, a sister came to care for the dying man. The visitor kept watching the sister work. He saw how tenderly she cared for her patient. He noticed how tenderly she washed the man and smiled at him. She didn't miss a detail in her attentive care for that dying man. I was also at the home for the dying that day.

The visitor, after carefully watching the sister, turned to me and said, "I came here today, not believing in God, with my heart full of hate." He then told me what his state of mind had been upon arriving at our home for the dying. "But now I am leaving here believing in God. I have seen the love of God in action. Through the hands of that sister—through her gestures, through her tenderness—which were so full of love for that wretched man, I have seen God's love descend upon him. Now I believe." I didn't even know who this visitor was at the time, or that he was an atheist.

This is what I expect from our co-workers. Do you want to do the same thing for those around you? You need to be united to Christ. You need prayer. Your service must come from a heart filled with God. This is not impossible. It is possible with the one who can do everything. Without him, we can do nothing. "Through him, in him and with him," just as we pray at Mass, we will be able to serve.

With God, nothing is impossible. Our sisters are living proof of that. When I watch them, I perceive the infinite greatness of God, a greatness that we can tap into. I see how he can work through us. Because you and I have nothing on our own we need him. As the Bible says, God waits and looks. Will we respond?

Just consider what God has accomplished through the sisters and the co-workers scattered throughout the world. We must ponder it in order to admire the greatness of God shown among us. This is not pride. It takes humility to recognize the greatness of God shining through us. Boasting of our greatness before men is pride. Great humility arises when we recognize that it is God's kindness and his greatness that shows through our hands, our work, and our love because that is the simple truth. Jesus is the truth that must be shared. All those who have witnessed our work, have been able to see that God is the source. Just as Jesus said, "Likewise, when men see your good deeds, they will give praise to your Father who is in heaven."

Accepting the Brothers and Sisters

This is one of the reasons why I accept all of the distinctions and honors that are continually being bestowed on me from one place or another. They don't affect me deeply. It's not a matter of it going in one ear and out the other. I always prefer to take things into my heart rather than having them fade away. It is something that comes with our work, but it doesn't *stop with me.* When an honor is bestowed, it isn't just for me.

I am sure that what just happened at Cambridge wasn't intended simply for me. Personally I felt like a small, weak child surrounded by an immense crowd of poor from everywhere. By bestowing an honor on me, they bestowed it also on you, on each of the sisters, and on each of the poor. Those at that great university know that every act of love must be shared, that you and I depend upon and support one another in our work. They also know that we are aware of the plight of the poor in the world, that we consider them our brothers and sisters. This is what makes many fall to their knees and encourages them to accept their brothers and sisters in the poor. That is why I showed my gratitude. Thinking of you and in the name of all of you, I said, "I accept." Otherwise the honor would have no meaning, as I said the other day at Cambridge when I addressed those who had assembled: "You know full well that I have not studied theology. I just simply try always to live it out." I wanted to make it clear that I was unqualified for what the academic world calls an honorary degree as a Doctor of Divinity.[10]

In reality, the event was a gift from God. And it was not just for me personally but for you, for the sisters and for our poor. We must appreciate and accept it with all humility of heart, so that we can offer it to Jesus. After all, it belongs to him. All glory and honor are his. We must let Jesus use us as he sees fit. In that way, every aspect of our life of prayer, of fundraising, and of feeding and clothing the poor complement each other. They cannot be separated. One cannot be done without the other. None of them can be done without prayer. Your generosity and your sacrifices must be the fruit of your prayer life.

Faith, we must remember, is a gift from God. One of our co-workers asked me once, "Do you want us to become Catholics like you?" I answered, "I would like to give you the treasure that I possess, but it is not in my hands to give it to anyone, because it is a gift from God. What I am doing is giving you the opportunity to do works of charity. Through these works, you come closer to God because works of charity bring you closer to God. When God comes to you or you go to God, then you will have the chance to accept him or reject him. Accepting him is the gift of faith."

Giving Jesus to Others

We should not be afraid to give Jesus to others. We should not be afraid to put our love into action. We should not be afraid to pray, to work, and to make our work a prayer. This is what a distinguished person in India said, "When I see the sisters in the streets of Calcutta, I always have the impression that Jesus Christ has come again into the world and that he is again going about, doing good works through the sisters." These words, expressed in such a beautiful way, are moving to me. I like to repeat them to everyone, especially to you, my coworkers. Through your deeds done to help the poor, Christ is going about doing good. Those who see us will see Christ in us.

EIGHT

The Poor Are Rich in Love

Loving and Responding to the Poor

Let's say a prayer that we know by heart in the Missionaries of Charity. Let's say it for our people who, as Brother Andrew[1] says, have given us a reason to gather and work together:

Make us worthy, Lord, to serve our brothers and sisters scattered throughout the entire world who live and die in poverty and hunger. Through the service of our hands, give them their daily bread; and by our understanding love, give them peace and joy.

Lord, make me an instrument of your peace;
where there is hatred, let me sow love;
where there is injury, pardon;
where there is doubt, faith;

_____

This talk was given to the Ladies of Charity in Los Angeles on October 3, 1973. This congregation was co-founded by St. Vincent de Paul. Hence, there is a reference to him later in Mother Teresa's address.

where there is despair, hope;
where there is darkness, light;
where there is sadness, joy.
O divine master, grant that I may not so much seek
to be consoled as to console;
to be understood as to understand;
to be loved as to love;
for it is in giving that we receive;
it is in pardoning that we are pardoned;
it is in dying that we are born to eternal life.
Amen.

In prayer I asked our Lady what I should say to you when an overwhelming thought came to me from above: that Mary is the first lady of charity. Yet before she became the first lady of charity, she emptied herself and submitted to the Lord as his handmaid. And the first thing she did when she found herself full of grace after the annunciation was to go in haste to share Jesus with St. John the Baptist and his parents.

I believe that is what you are all called to do as men and women of charity, as carriers of God's love. This is also our mission as Missionaries of Charity. I hope the day will come when we may become the carriers of God's love to everyone. All this means that the beautiful work you are accomplishing among the poor and for the poor is a privilege and a gift.

As I recall, St. Vincent de Paul used to say to his young postulants: "Don't forget that the poor are your masters. Pledge your love and obedience to them." I am convinced that if we approach the poor with the desire to give them God, he will bless our work. If we desire to bring them the joy of Christ which is our strength and help bring Christ into their homes, he will be with us. If we give the poor the chance to find Jesus and his loving kindness in us, soon the world will be overflowing with peace and love. The poor are great people. They are also very kind people. They teach us much.

The last time there were a great number of refugees from Bangladesh in India,[2] the Indian government allowed sisters to come from all over to help us in our service to the poor. Sisters from fifteen different congregations came. Our little congregation, which was so young and so small then, was like a drop in the ocean compared to all those larger and more established congregations.

Nevertheless, none of our sisters went elsewhere to live as guests of the other congregations. In fact, sisters from the other congregations wanted to share our life of poverty and prayer, so they could understand the poor better. They wanted to know what poverty is. They wanted to know the poor so as to love them and serve them better. And they lived with us for six months. Before leaving us, each of them personally expressed her gratitude, typically saying, "I have received much more than what I have given. I will never be the same." I have heard news that those sisters returned to their congregations much more conscious of the problems facing those who feel unloved, those who are neglected. They learned much from the poor.

We know that poverty means, first of all, to be hungry for bread, to need clothing, and not have a home. But there is a far greater kind of poverty. It means being unwanted, unloved, and neglected. It means having no one to call your own.

Hungry for God

We may experience this kind of poverty even in our own homes. Often it is difficult for us to smile, even at our children, our husband, or our wife. Our young boys and girls then sense the lack of affection around them. Here is where love really starts. Love should start at home. We must give Jesus absolute reign in our homes. Once we have Jesus with us, then we can give him to others.

Today the world is hungry for God. You and I can bring him to others, as long as we ourselves have understood the love of Christ. Our brothers and sisters work for the poorest of the poor. They work for the unwanted, the unloved, the sick, the dying, the lepers, and the abandoned children in our midst.

I can assure you that in these twenty-three years of our service as an order,[3] I have never heard a poor person complain, curse, or express sadness. The greatness of our people is that they know how to accept things in life.

We have many, many lepers who need care. You would be surprised to learn what happens when we ask the sisters of our congregation who among them is willing to work with the lepers. They all raise their hands. Even though the lepers are grotesquely disfigured and almost repulsive to look at, Christ is in them. He has said, "You did it to me. I was sick, naked, given up for dead; and you did it to me."

Giving All to Christ and His Poor

Jesus will not deceive us. He tells us, "I was hungry and you gave me to eat." Every time we are faced with such sacrifices for the poor, every time we are concerned about the poor—whether they are near or far away—we do it all for him. Every time you sacrifice something at great cost—every time you renounce something that appeals to you for the sake of the poor—you are feeding a hungry Christ. You are clothing his nakedness. You are offering shelter to a homeless Christ. You do this when you help in caring for the poor around you.

There are hundreds of sisters who belong to the Order of the Daughters of Divine Charity. They are scattered throughout India. We work closely with them because we share the same ideals, except that our habits are different. We serve the same loving master. All of us are in contact with the same body of Jesus Christ. It is all God's work.

Every time you are concerned for the poor and you make sacrifices for them—wherever you serve them you are really doing it for Christ. That is why I feel overwhelmed with gratitude for the opportunity to be with you. I want personally to thank you for all that you have done for our poor. I thank you for all the prayers and sacrifices that you have made. But do not forget that it isn't enough to give money. The money will come. Money is not the hard part. We have to give until it hurts. We need to give from the resources we would like to keep for ourselves. We need to give to the point of sacrificing. We must give something that we find hard to give up.

That is what is so beautiful about the poor. We have a home for alcoholics in Melbourne, a place for homeless alcoholics. One of those rescued had been badly beaten by another. It seemed to me that the police should be called in. We called the police who came and questioned the man, "Who did this to you?" But it became clear that he would never tell the truth, that he would never reveal the name of the guilty party. The police had no alternative but to leave without finding out. Then I asked the man, "Why did you refuse to give the name of the man who hurt you in this way?" He looked at me and said, "His suffering would not have lessened mine."

How beautiful and great is our people's love! The ongoing miracle of love is constantly being sowed among our poor. We call them poor, but they are really rich in love and mercy.

Our sisters, as I think you know, try to live a life of poverty. We need to experience what poverty is so we can understand the poor. Knowing them leads us to love them, and loving them leads us to serve them.

In fact, we have something special in our congregation. We have a fourth vow where we profess to offer wholehearted and free service to the poorest of the poor. We receive freely and we give freely, out of pure love for God. We don't have any income. I sometimes find myself overwhelmed by the amount of things that we receive. Money rather frightens me and it causes me to worry, especially when it comes to us in such large amounts. Still, thanks be to God! In the same way we receive it, we give of it. It is wonderful to see how money comes to us.

When we opened our home in New York, the late Cardinal Terence Cooke was very concerned about the prospect of having to send us a fixed amount every month for the livelihood of the sisters. He was a man who loved the sisters very much. I didn't want to hurt his feelings, but I found it very hard to explain to him that we work only for the love of God. We simply couldn't accept any fixed amount for our living expenses. I explained to him the only way that I could. I told him, "Your Eminence, I don't think God is going to go bankrupt here in New York."

God has proven this to us time and again. We continually keep on receiving help from on high. I arrived here without even a dollar, and I am leaving here with such a large amount of money that I don't even want to count it. It has been simply marvelous.

I believe that the most important thing is for us to love Jesus, then to love one another—ourselves and the members of our families—and to show our love for the poor. What is important is that we are able to smile at one another in our families. With a generous and cheerful smile, we should be able to accept everything that happens in our families, both the joyful things and the sad things.

I believe that the commitment spouses profess in their marriage vows is important. They accept each other in good times and in bad times. I think that this is something that we should always try to do with a smile. And it really helps if we can then do the same in the homes of the poorest of the poor.

It's possible that in the apartment or house across from yours, there is someone who is blind. Perhaps there is a blind man who would be thrilled if you would go over and read the newspaper to him. It's possible that there is a family that needs something that seems insignificant to you, something as simple as having someone babysit their child for half an hour.

There are so many little things that are so small many people almost forget about them. But for you, as sons and daughters of charity, these aren't small things. They show your love for Christ. And this is what I am asking of you. Place yourselves at the service of the poor. Above all, do it right where you are and love them from the heart.

NINE

Smiling at Christ in His Poor

Hungry for God and His Peace

I thank God for the Nobel Peace Prize. And a prayer of thanksgiving wells up in my heart. In fact, I think it is always so beautiful for us to say the Prayer of St. Francis of Assisi. I am so fond of this prayer. We Missionaries of Charity say this prayer every day after Holy Communion. And we find that it speaks from the heart for each one of us. I happen to think that when St. Francis composed this prayer, the difficulties that he had to face hundreds of years ago must have been very similar to the difficulties of those of us who find this prayer so in tune with our own feelings and needs today. I think some of you know it by heart. Let's pray it together.

Let us give thanks to God for the opportunity that he has given us in our day. Let us thank him for this

The talk was given by Mother Teresa in Oslo, Norway on December 11, 1979. The previous day she had received the Nobel Peace Prize, which she had been awarded on October 17 of the same year.

peace prize which reminds us that we have been created to live in peace. Jesus became man to bring that good news to the poor. Being God, he became like us in every way except sin. And he proclaimed clearly that he had come to bring good news. That good news was God's peace to all men of good will. That peace is something which is fundamental to the satisfaction of our most basic desires. It is a peace of the heart.

God so loved the world that he gave us his Son. This act of love was a gift. It is just like saying that God gave until it hurt, since he loved the world so much that he gave us his Son through Mary. And what did Mary do? As soon as Jesus came into her life, she ran to share the good news. And when she came into her cousin's house, the child in Elizabeth's womb leapt for joy. The little unborn baby was the first messenger of peace. John the Baptist recognized the Prince of Peace. He recognized that Christ had come to bring good news to you and me.

As if that were not enough—as if it were not enough to have become man—Jesus died on the cross to show us his great love. He died for you and me. He died for that leper. He died for that man who is starving not only in the streets of Calcutta but in Africa, in New York, in London, and in Oslo. And Jesus insisted that we love one another the way he loves us. This message is clear in the Gospels: "Love one another as I have loved you. As the Father has loved me so I have loved you." His Father loved us in him so much that he gave him up for us.

And the more we love each other, the more we should give of ourselves to one another until it hurts. We cannot say, "I love God, but I don't love my neighbor." St. John tells us that he who says he loves God but not his neighbor, is a liar. How can you love God whom you do not see, if you don't love the neighbor whom you do see—the neighbor you know and live with every day?

It is very important to understand that love has to hurt to be true. It hurt Jesus to love us. It truly hurt him. And to insure that we would be reminded of his great love, he made himself the Bread of Life to satisfy our hunger for his love. We hunger for God because we have been created to love. We have been created in his image and likeness. We have been created to love and to be loved. For that reason, he became man to make it possible for us to love as he has loved us.

Jesus became the hungry, the naked, the homeless, the sick, the imprisoned, the forsaken, and the unwanted in our midst. And he says, "And you did it unto me." They are hungry for our love. That is the hunger of our poor. That is the hunger that you and I must meet, because it may even exist in our own homes.

See, here is where love finds its place. Poverty comes into our homes to give us the chance to love. Perhaps in our own families, there is someone who feels lonely, who is sick, or who is overburdened with worry. Are we there, open and willing to offer support and affection? Are you, mothers, available to your children?

I was surprised to find out how many young people in the slums, both boys and girls, are involved with drugs. I have tried to find out why. "Why is this happening?" I asked.

The answer was, "There is no one at home to love them. Parents are too busy and don't have time for them. Young parents are so involved in social commitments and activities that their children go out into the streets and get mixed up in something which is bad for them." Here we are talking about peace, and these are the very things that shatter peace.

Abortion Destroys Life

I think that abortion is the greatest destroyer of peace today precisely because it is war. It is killing. It is a deliberate and calculated murder carried out with the mother's collaboration. We read in Scripture what God clearly says about this: "Even if a mother should forget her child, I shall not forsake you. You are in the palm of my hand." God has us in the very palm of his hand. And that is what strikes me. Even if a mother could forget her child which seems impossible, "I will not forsake you." Today abortion is the greatest and most effective destroyer of peace.

We were wanted by our parents. We wouldn't be here if our parents hadn't wanted us. We want and love our own children. But what happens to millions of other children? Many people are concerned about children in India and Africa where many die from malnutrition or starvation or other causes. But there are millions who are dying with the express consent of their own mothers.

There is simply no greater destroyer of peace in our day. If a mother can kill her own child, what is the difference with my killing of you or your killing of me? There isn't any! In India and everywhere else, this is my fervent plea. Let's save the children!

This is the International Year of the Child.[1] What

have we done for our children? At the beginning of the year, whenever I had the chance, I spoke out and said: "Let's make this the year in which every child, born or yet to be born, feels wanted. The Year of the Child is coming to an end. Have we managed to make children more wanted and loved?"

I am going to talk to you about a surprising event. We are fighting abortion with adoptions. We have saved thousands upon thousands of lives. We have sent word to all the clinics, the hospitals, and the police stations: please don't destroy the baby. We will take care of him. That way, at any hour of the day or night, there is usually someone who comes. Quite often it is a single woman who calls us, knowing that we will take care of her baby and find him a good home. We have a large number of couples who are childless, which for us, is a blessing from God. They can adopt the babies who are in need of a home.

We are carrying out something else that is very beautiful. We are teaching natural family planning to our beggars, our lepers, our slum dwellers, and our homeless street people. In Calcutta alone, in the last six years (I repeat that in Calcutta alone) we now have 61,273 less children in our families than would have been the case precisely because they have practiced the natural method of abstinence and self-control. And they have done so without sacrificing their love for one another. The method we teach them is very beautiful and simple.

Our poor understand it. Do you know what many of them have told me? "Our family is in good health. We are united, and we can have a child whenever we want to have one." It's that clear and straightforward for these people who live in the streets. I believe that if our people can do this, how much more can all the rest of us! We can use the means of natural family planning and decide not to destroy the life that God has created in us!

The poor are such great people! They can teach us so many beautiful things! The other day, one of our poor came to thank us. He said, "You people, who have taken the vow of chastity, are the best ones to teach us natural family planning. That's because it isn't anything but self-control without forsaking our love for one another in marriage." I think he said something very beautiful.

Yet these are people who sometimes have nothing to eat and many times have nowhere to live. But they are still great people! The poor are marvelous people.

To Die Like an Angel

One evening we went out and rescued four people off the streets. One of them was in a desperate condition. I told the sisters, "You take care of the others. I will care for this one who is worse off." I did for her everything that my love could do. I put her into bed, and I saw a beautiful smile light up her face. She squeezed my hand and only managed to say two words: "Thank you." And then she closed her eyes.

I couldn't help but ask myself there beside her body, "What would I have said if I had been in her place?" My answer was very simple. I would have tried to draw attention to myself. I would have said that I was hungry, that I was dying, that I was cold. Or I would have said that this or that part of my body hurt or something like that. But she gave me much more. She gave me her grateful love. And she died with a smile on her face.

Just like that man whom we rescued from among the debris in the gutter, the one who was half-eaten by worms, this woman responded in grateful love. That man told us, "I have lived like an animal in the street, but I am going to die like an angel surrounded by love and care." It was marvelous to witness the greatness of that man who could talk like that, who could die that way without cursing anyone, without lashing out at anyone, without drawing any comparisons. He died like an angel. That is the greatness of our people! And that is why we need to take Jesus at his word when he says, "I was hungry, naked, homeless, unwanted, and deprived of love and care. And you did it to me."

The Neighbor Next Door to Us

I believe that we are not simply social workers. In the eyes of others, we may be doing social work. But we are really contemplatives in the heart of the world because we are touching the body of Christ twenty-four hours a day. We spend twenty-four hours a day in his presence.

You, too, must try to bring the presence of God to your families, for the family that prays together, stays together. I think that just being together and loving one another brings peace and joy. It strengthens the bond between family members in the home. That is the way to overcome all the evil that is in the world.

There is so much suffering, so much hate, so much sorrow! We can be real pillars in our homes through our prayers and sacrifices. Love begins at home. It isn't how much we do, but how much love we put into what we do that really counts. That is because our actions are focused on God. It doesn't matter how much we do, but how much love we put into our actions, for his love is infinite.

I have received countless signs of affection from you. I have been surrounded by an atmosphere of love: a love based on true understanding. I have the impression that every person in Africa and in India is someone who is special to you. Just a few hours ago I confided to a sister that I feel at home. I feel like I am in the convent with the sisters, as if I were really with them in Calcutta. Yes, I feel perfectly at home as I speak to you.

I want you to go and find the poor in your homes. Above all, your love has to start there. I want you to be the good news to those around you. I want you to be concerned about your next-door neighbor. Do you know who your neighbor is? Who are your neighbors?

The Passion of Christ

Remember where your love starts: in the home.

I want you to know that I am very grateful for what I have received from you.[2] It has been a marvelous experience being with you. Soon I will be on my way home, and I will be taking your love home with me. I know that you have not given leftovers. You have given with sacrifice.

Even your little children have brought their gifts of love. This has been a surprise for me. It will be a great joy to the children who are suffering from hunger to know that other children—who have the same needs for love, affection, and tenderness—have received abundantly from their parents and give so freely of themselves. Let's give thanks to God for having given us this opportunity to know each other. By knowing each other we have drawn closer to one another in Christ. Through your generosity, we are going to be able to help children around the world because—as you well know—our sisters are scattered all over the world serving the children of the poor.

With the Nobel Peace Prize that I have been given, I will try to build homes for many people who are without shelter. I am convinced that love begins at home. So if we can build more homes for the poor, I think that will make even more love possible among our people. This compassionate love will help us to bring peace, to be the good news to the poor. First, we must bring peace to the poor in our own families. After that, we must bring this peace to the poor in our own country, and from there to the whole world.

To be capable of doing this, our sisters' lives must be saturated with prayer. They have to live completely surrendered to Christ, so they can understand and share this peace that God brings. There is so much suffering today.

I have the impression that the passion of Christ is being re-lived everywhere. Are we willing to share in this passion? Are we willing to share people's sufferings, not only in poor countries but all over the world?

It seems to me that this great poverty of suffering in the West is much harder to solve. When I pick up some starving person off the street and offer him a bowl of rice or a piece of bread, I can satisfy his hunger. But a person that has been beaten or feels unwanted or unloved or fearful or rejected by society—that person experiences a kind of poverty that is much more painful and deep. Its cure is much more difficult to find. Our sisters work among these kinds of people in the West. They share in the passion of Christ.

Smiling at Our Brothers and Sisters

You need to remember us in your prayers, so that we can be that good news to the suffering poor. We simply can't do it without your help. You need to do the same in your own country. You need to make an effort to know your poor. It is possible that your people enjoy material security, that they don't need anything of that sort.[3] But I think that if you look inside your own homes, you may notice how hard it is for you to smile at one another sometimes! And yet smiling is the beginning of love. Let's be willing to smile at one another. Yes, a smile is the beginning of love. And once we begin to love one another, the desire to do something more naturally follows.

So I ask you to pray for our sisters and for me, for our brothers[4] and our co-workers, who are scattered far and wide around the world. Pray that we remain faithful to God's gift to us: to love him and serve him in the poor. The work we have carried out would not have been possible if you hadn't shared in it through your prayers, your gifts, and your never-failing generosity.

I don't want you to give me what you have left over. I want you to give from your want until you really feel it! The other day I received fifteen dollars from a man who has been paralyzed for twenty years. The paralysis only allows him the use of his right hand. The only company he tolerates is tobacco. He told me, "I have stopped smoking for a week. I'm sending you the money I've saved from cigarettes." It must have been a horrible sacrifice for him.

But look at the beauty of his act of sharing. I bought bread with his money, and I gave it to those who were hungry. So both the giver and those who received experienced joy: the paralytic in giving and the poor in receiving. This is something all of us need to learn. The chance to share our love with others is a gift from God. May it be for us just as it was for Jesus. Let's love one another as he has loved us. Let's love one another with undivided love. Let's experience the joy of loving God and loving one another.

The Power of True Peace

Let us keep the joy of loving Jesus in our hearts. And let's share that joy with everyone we meet. Passing on joy is something which is very natural. We have no reason for not being joyful, since Christ is with us. Christ is in our hearts. Christ is in the poor we meet. Christ is in the smile we give to others, and he is in the smile we receive from others.

Let's concentrate on a worthwhile goal: that no child be unwanted, that no person go unloved. And let's not stop smiling at whomever we meet, especially when it's hard to smile.

I'll never forget some time ago when around fourteen professors from different universities in the United States came to visit one of our homes in

Calcutta. We were talking about the visit we had just made to the home for the poor who are dying. (In Calcutta we have a home for the dying where we have taken in thirty-six thousand people from off the streets. Some eighteen thousand of them have had a very beautiful death. They have gone home to God.) These professors came to see me and we were talking about love and kindness. One of them asked me, "Mother, tell us something that we can remember."

I told them, "Smile at each other. Take some time for each other in your families. Smile."

Then one of them asked me, "Are you married?" I said, "Yes, and sometimes I find it very difficult to smile at Jesus because he can be so demanding."

It's true. But that is where you can see love best. When it is most demanding and you give cheerfully in spite of that, that is love at its best.

I think there is something that can make us live joyfully. It is that Jesus is with us. He loves us. If each one of us would simply remember that God loves us and is giving us the chance to love others in that love—not so much in big things but in the little things of life—our countries could become full of God's love. And how beautiful it would be if the power of peace would go forth and destroy the power to make war and take life. How great it would be to see the joy of life break forth into the lives of the unborn! If you become this kind of torch lit for peace in the world, then indeed the Nobel Peace Prize will be a true gift from the Norwegian people. God bless you![5]

TEN

The Joy and Freedom of Poverty

Knowing the Poor

Let us give thanks for the privilege God has given you and I in allowing us to serve him in the poor. Let's also thank our people—the poor—for accepting our service. If they didn't accept us, there wouldn't be any Missionaries of Charity or co-workers. And it is our co-workers who, through their sacrifices and prayers, never stop helping and encouraging the sisters in their work. They perform that important service for each one of us.

There are even contemplative communities that have adopted our sisters. This has caused a marvelous sharing among our communities of co-workers. Some contemplative communities offer their prayers and sacrifices for us, while we offer our work and prayers for them.[1] In this way, we have become a new source of

---

This address was given by Mother Teresa to her co-workers in Liverpool, England, on September 23, 1978 when she opened a home for her Missionaries of Charity in that city.

life for them, and they have become a new source of strength for us. We feel especially indebted to our sick and chronically ill co-workers.[2] Quite often when the work is very difficult and I see such intense suffering in our people, the thought of our sick co-workers offering up their pain for the suffering around us makes me see that they are an immense gift sent from heaven.

We should gather to give thanks to God for what he has done in us, with us, and through us. We thank him for having used you and us to be his love and mercy. God is still love, and he still loves the world. We believe that God so loved the world that he gave his only begotten Son. And God so loves the world today that he gives you and me to love the world, so that we may be his love and his mercy. What a beautiful thought and conviction for us, that we can be that love and mercy right in our homes, above all. Then we can be that love and mercy for our next-door neighbors and for our neighbors down the street.

But do we know our neighbors? Do we know the poor in our neighborhood? It's easier for us to talk and talk about the poor in far-away places. We are often surrounded by the sick and the abandoned. We are often among people who are despised, outcast, and depressed. We have many elderly whom we don't even know. At times, we don't even have the time to smile at these people.

The Hunger for Love

As Jesus' co-workers, one thing we have to learn is to sow joy. We don't need bombs or weapons to bring peace to the world. We need that love and compassion that we ask for every day. We need a truly compassionate love—a compassion and love that bring joy and peace. The world is hungry for God.

When Jesus came into the world, he loved it so much that he gave his life for it. He wanted to satisfy our hunger for God. And what did he do? He made himself the Bread of Life. He became small, fragile, and defenseless for us. Bits of bread can be so small that even a baby can chew it, even a dying person can eat it. He became the Bread of Life to satisfy our hunger for God, our hunger for love.

As if that were not enough, he himself took on our human condition. He became hungry. He became naked. He became the poor one dying in our streets, so that we could satisfy our hunger for human love by loving him. This is not something which is imaginary. It is not something out of the ordinary. God comes to us in human love so that we can love him with our hearts. He wants us to love him in those who are hungry, in those who are naked, in those who are homeless. This is what you and I are called to do. We must learn to pray steadfastly for this call.

The work that each one of you carries out in your families for those you love is an expression of your love for God. Love starts at home. For your love to be real, it cannot waver at home.

Recently a real windfall of charity was experienced throughout Bengal. Food and clothing arrived from everywhere. It came from schools, men, women, and children to be distributed during the recent monsoon disaster. The monsoon was something terrible, but it brought about something very beautiful. It brought about sharing. It brought about the concern and awareness that our brothers and sisters were suffering because of a natural disaster. And many people decided to do something to help them. There were people who prepared meals in their homes to share with those in need. It was something very beautiful to witness that such terrible suffering could help bring about so much good in so many people.

A Word About Sharing

I don't want you to give to us from your abundance. I don't need money from your abundance. Instead, I ask that you share in our work. I ask that you lend your hands in understanding. Come and help care for our needy. Come and see. This very day I have found myself with some of our people who came to one of our homes to eat. They are such kind people! They give thanks from the very bottom of their hearts. They have nothing. It isn't that we have given them any extras, just some sandwiches and a cup of tea. Very little! But it has been enough to give them the sense that they are loved, that there is a place where they can come. They are being offered a concrete expression of love. They are being taken into account. This is something that I wanted to share with you.

I think that we need to grow more as co-workers, taking the place that is rightfully ours. Sharing is the distinctive note of co-workers. I repeat that I don't want you to give to me from your abundance. I want you to give with the attitude of that little boy who said, "I will not eat sugar for three days. I will give it to Mother Teresa." Little things like that make all the difference. I am convinced that for us as adults that seems like something insignificant. But we forget that that child loved with a big heart. And there are so many things that happen around us that go almost un-noticed.

Children in England have been doing this kind of thing for the last twenty years.[3] They have been giving bread to the children of Calcutta. More than four thousand Indian children receive their daily ration of bread, thanks to the generosity of these children. It is something truly beautiful.

The children from Denmark provide them with a glass of milk. The children from Germany offer them daily vitamins. At times, some donors are even sick children themselves. Quite often it is a matter of small things. But these children put so much love into their giving and receiving that they help each other to grow in love!

Thanks be to God for your families. Try to find room for God in your families. I know what I am saying. If you are capable of bringing prayer back into your homes, you will be equally capable of overcoming all of the hardships that afflict the world.

There is so much suffering, so much hatred, and so many upheavals. Why? Because family life is breaking up. And when there is no family life, vocations become scarce, for vocations come from the family. We need the best gift you can give us: your children.[4] When some bishops ask me, "Mother, send us your sisters," I tell them, "Give me your daughters and I will give you sisters."

I am very willing to increase the number of sisters in your dioceses if you will give me more postulants.

After they profess their final vows, they can return to love and serve your people that are hungry for God, people like the ones I see all around me each day.

This is what I want you to feel and experience. You must be able to understand what I am telling you. I had to experience it before I was able to understand. The same thing happens to each one of you. You have to start by experiencing it firsthand in your own homes. You must make "Nazareths" of your own homes and families. There love, peace, joy, and unity must reign. Then you will see what I have described to you in the faces of your own family and communicate it to those around you.

The Greatest Gift from God

The other day some of the sisters were telling me that they had gone somewhere (in New York City), and they were told that someone had died in an apartment. No one knew when, and they had to force the door open to get in. What did they find? Rats were eating the body. It was a woman. The sisters tried to find out who she was, whose daughter or mother or wife. But no one knew anything about that woman except her apartment number. What tremendous poverty! Imagine the loneliness, the feeling of knowing that she was unwanted, despised, and neglected! That is what we as co-workers must fight in our own families.

We must ask for the grace to love one another. As Jesus said, "Love one another as I have loved you." To be capable of doing that, our sisters live a life of prayer and sacrifice. That is why we start our day with prayer,

Holy Communion, and meditation. Every evening we also have an hour of worship before the Blessed Sacrament. We have permission from our bishop for this time of adoration before the sacrament. This hour of intimacy with Jesus is something very beautiful. It is the greatest gift that God can give us.

Wherever you find yourself, if you are free and you feel the need for Jesus, we have daily worship from 6:30 to 7:30 P.M. in our homes. You are cordially invited to come. Or if it is more practical, go to your own church. Wherever you find yourself, try to begin doing this. Try to put worship into practice in your life. Be alone with Jesus. You will notice a change in your life, in your family, in your parish, and in your environment.

This is something that we should be concerned about as co-workers. We need to soak up the tender love of Jesus that our people experience when they sense that God loves them. We need to extend to each and every one the assurance that God loves them.

Let's fix our eyes on the cross. What do we see? We see his head bent down to kiss us. Look at his hands. They say, "I love you!" We see his arms stretched out on the cross as if to embrace us. We see his heart opened wide to receive us. That is the cross, which is represented by the crucifix that most of us have in our homes. Each time we glance at it, it should help us to fall in love with Christ. It should help us to love him with sincerity of heart. What greater love is there than God's love for each one of us? His love isn't a fantasy. It is real.

Strive to soak up the simplicity and purity of Christ.

Try to be more in tune with God and more open to him, so that you will be able to see his face. Jesus said, "Blessed are the pure of heart, for they will see God." We need to have an open heart to be able to see God in others. Let's pray for the grace we need. Pray for us so that we may be able to accomplish God's work with plenty of love. Pray for us that we won't spoil it. Pray that you and I may really be one. I consider you as our co-workers an integral part of us, a very intimate part of our congregation.

The Gift of Love

We cannot be divided. We must all work together. Co-workers cannot be considered something which is apart from the rest of the congregation. We are all one. In this unity, where two or three are gathered, Christ is there with us. To achieve this unity, the sisters profess the vow of chastity. That means loving Christ with an undivided love in the freedom to be poor and in total surrender through obedience.

This is why the fourth vow we profess in our congregation is so important. We commit ourselves to offer wholehearted, free service to the poorest of the poor. Through this vow we freely commit ourselves to the poorest of the poor. We are at their service. We become totally dependent on God's providence, and that providence has been wonderful to us. Christ has kept his word. We are more important to his Father than the lilies of the field and the birds of the air.

It is really true. We have no fixed income of any sort. Even so, from the moment we arrive at some place, we are continually showered with gifts. I have told the sisters on occasion, "If we continue at this rate, we will soon need a new building." It is truly beautiful! A sister goes shopping at the market and returns with the same amount of money in her pocket. The same thing happens in London and elsewhere.

The other day I went to Hyderabad[5] to open a new center. A Hindu gentleman, who I had never seen before, was waiting for us with a surprise. He had decided to donate his house as a free gift to the sisters. It was a beautiful house with a garden and everything else one could need. He had put it in our name without any strings attached. That is something beautiful that is beginning to happen more and more frequently.

I suppose that you know about Imperial Chemical Industries.[6] They gave us a factory that used to manufacture all kinds of chemical products. I told them that this factory is now going to produce love, chemicals of love to help all sorts of people. And it really is producing love because so many people are becoming committed to serving the poor.

There are young people who come from all over the world to spend two weeks or a month working at the humblest of jobs out of love for others. They pick up all sorts of people off the streets for us, but they do it with a great deal of love. I feel unable to explain adequately what happens to those who lovingly serve the poor and what also happens to the people who are lovingly served. These homes of ours have become homes in which treasures of the kingdom are hidden.

In the same way, I hope that all the homes that we have opened will be our gift to you. They are gifts of love for your people. Through them, we hope to welcome many men and women in different areas who have nowhere to go because no one wants them. They have no one, and we want to offer them a home, a gift of love. We want to offer them a home where they can come and feel comfortable. We want to offer them a place where they can be loved and cared for, where their needs will be met.

To Die Is to Go Home

The greatest gift that God can bestow on a family is to choose a son or a daughter for himself. You should encourage this, but it will not be possible for you if you don't pray. Let us pray then. Let's not pray long, drawn-out prayers, but let's pray short ones full of love. Prayer unites us with Christ. Simply open your hearts to him. Also, simply accept what he sends you. With a big smile, generously give him what he asks of you. You will soon realize that this is the best prayer that you can offer in your families. God will do the rest, never fear. Where God is, there is love; and where there is love, there always is an openness to serve.

As Christians, we have been created for great things. We have been created to be holy since we have been created in the image of God. So holiness is not a luxury for only a few, but it is a duty for everyone. There is nothing extraordinary about being holy. We have been created for that purpose. For that reason, when someone dies that person is meant to go home to God. That is where we are all meant to go. Death can be something beautiful. It is like going home. He who dies in God goes home even though we naturally miss the person who has gone. But it is something beautiful. That person has gone home to God.

When the Holy Father died, someone from England called me and asked me about him. I said that the Holy Father was just fine. Paul VI was a true saint! He was an authentic saint. He loved the poor, and he had a special love for the Missionaries of Charity. Now he has gone home to be with God, and we can pray for him.

The same holds true for each of us. So let's pray for one another. Let us pray that we may accomplish our life's mission which is to be holy. Let us pray that we will be the love and kindness of God in today's world.

I think you will be happy to know that in 1975 we celebrated the silver jubilee of our congregation. And in 1977 we celebrated the silver jubilee of the home for dying destitutes. In twenty-five years, we have picked up thirty-six thousand people from off the streets of Calcutta alone. And we know that seventeen thousand of them had a very beautiful death.

This year we celebrated the silver jubilee of the first group that started our congregation. That is why we have decided to give Jesus twenty-five new tabernacles; that is to say, twenty-five new homes. At this moment, we have founded eighteen, so you must pray for the other seven that are still to be built. It is very beautiful to confirm the desire of other people to share with us in this work. I never go to a new center without there being a tabernacle for the Blessed Sacrament, a ciborium, a chalice, and a monstrance on hand. We have these four things in our chapels to house the presence of Christ in our midst.

In Germany, the rumor began to circulate that I had

to open seven new homes. I received a telephone call from Germany. Several priests and a bishop had gotten together and had bought us seven tabernacles and seven chalices. As you can see then, I will just have to open the homes in God's time.

It is so wonderful to celebrate the silver jubilee by offering twenty-five tabernacles to Jesus! God has been so extraordinarily generous with us. We have many magnificent vocations. Let me express my deepest gratitude to all of you co-workers who help us with your prayers and your sacrifices in support of the sisters wherever they may be.

Poor by Choice

You must continue helping the sisters. I have just told the sisters that we must help our people when they come to us wanting to live a normal human life. We must give them the things they will need when they leave us. We do not need extraordinary things, but only what's necessary so that they may have a joyful life.

As we try to do this for our people, you must protect the poverty of the sisters. We have chosen to be poor. That doesn't mean that we cannot have material goods. In and of itself, it isn't bad to have things, but we have *chosen* not to have them. So you must help to protect us. For once the sisters abound with material goods, we will not have time to tenderly and lovingly care for the poorest of the poor. We will then be too busy caring for things instead of people. So we must continue to have as little as possible. That way Jesus can always come and live comfortably among us.

We must always be thankful to God for the wonderful work that he allows us to carry out in his name. As you know, we also have the Missionary Brothers of Charity.[7] They are doing a lot of good. The brothers are accomplishing a marvelous work. Two years ago we also started a contemplative branch of the Missionaries of Charity in New York.[8] We have a contemplative branch for the brothers in Rome as well. And what does this new group do?

They spend their days in prayer, in worship, in reparation, and in penance. They set aside two hours daily for work away from home among the poorest of the poor. They dedicate themselves to proclaiming the Word of God to the people that they meet, bringing the Word of God into their lives. These sisters wear white habits, just like our novices in New York.[9]

One day they went out and came across a man in the street who was very drunk. They thought that it was a good opportunity. The sisters said to each other, "Here is someone to whom we must bring the Word of God." As for the man, when he saw the sisters approaching he cried, "Go away! I'm not ready! I'm not ready!" When the sisters tried to come closer to him and say, "We are only two sisters," he replied, "No, no you're not. You are two angels from heaven. You have taken me by surprise, and I'm not ready yet." Amazingly, I think he was ready because after a while he came along with them. He made his confession and was reconciled to God.

Our sisters' work is marvelous in the contemplative branch. We need to pray that they may be faithful to this beautiful gift of constant union with Christ, which is also the gift of proclaiming Christ through his Word, just as we dedicate ourselves to proclaiming him through our deeds. They proclaim Christ through the Word of God.

Once again, I wish to thank you for the marvelous things that you are doing, for all the love you lavished on the sisters since they arrived. I haven't the slightest doubt about their staying with you and working among you. Protect and help them. Help them not to lose the joy of poverty. Help them to treasure the joy and freedom of poverty. For us, poverty is freedom. And it is absolute freedom. It is real joy because we have chosen to be poor. Our poor are not poor by choice, but we have chosen to be poor. This is our joy.

Pray for us so that we may not fail in our commitment, so that we may not be unfaithful. Pray that all of us together—co-workers and Missionaries of Charity—may be united as if we were one person and give glory to God. May all who see our good works give glory to the Father. May God bless you!

ELEVEN

True Religious Freedom

By assuming your office in the name of God, you recognized his supreme rights over our country and our peoples. How beautiful that was! Now I am afraid that you are not accomplishing what you promised to do on that day. So I fear for my people.

You have allowed abortion, and this has sown hatred in the nation. If a mother can kill her own child, why can we not kill whoever gets in our way? It seems to me that you do not realize what abortion is doing to your people. Immorality is increasing. Many homes are breaking up. There is an alarming increase in the number of cases of insanity among mothers who kill their innocent children. The best people in this land are beginning to suffer from this trauma that can cause even more harm.

Mr. Morarji Desai, perhaps you will find yourself

This letter was written and personally delivered by Mother Teresa to then Prime Minister of India, Morarji Desai, on March 26, 1979. It was written in response to a proposed law dealing with religious freedom. If it had been passed, it would have been disastrous for Christianity and other religions in India.

face to face with God soon.¹ I do not know what
explanation you are going to give him for destroying
the lives of so many innocent, unborn children. When
you find yourself before the judgment seat of God, he
will judge you for the good that you have done and for
the evil that took place during your term in office as
prime minister.

Once more I want to tell you that never for an instant
have we stopped contributing our grain of salt to
whatever is of spiritual or material benefit for the
people. Being aware of the serious problem that
uncontrolled population growth poses, we have had at
our disposal the most honest and effective means of
controlling population growth in India. We have
enthusiastically worked to support natural family
planning. We have accomplished this effectively with
legitimate methods that support the family without
destroying innocent lives.

In Calcutta alone at the present time, we run 102
centers where spouses are taught natural birth control
that supports their love for one another and for their
children. In the last years 11,701 Hindu families,
5,568 Muslim families, and 4,341 Christian families
have made use of our natural family planning centers.
A total of 21,610 families—thinking of themselves,
their children, and their country—have contributed to
decreasing the population by about seven thousand
children, without killing anyone. They have based this
control on the foundations of love, life, and country. I
hope that God will shower his blessings upon all the
children of India and upon us.

After much prayer and no small time spent in doing
sacrifices, I am writing to ask you to stop. Please pray

to God before taking this step that can destroy the happiness and the freedom of our people.[2] You know better than I that our people are God-fearing and can easily experience his living presence. Today our people feel insecure because the very nature of their freedom of conscience is being attacked.

Religion is not something that you and I can dictate. Religion is the worship of God, and therefore it is a matter of conscience. Each one of us must decide how we are going to worship. In my case, the religion that I live and practice is Roman Catholicism. It is my life, my joy, and the greatest proof of God's love for me. No one can deny that I dearly love my people more than myself and that logically I want to share the joy of having this treasure with them. But it does not depend upon me. I cannot force anyone to accept my religion—just as no man, no law, and no government can legally demand that anyone reject a religion that promises them peace, joy, and love. It is said that Mahatma Gandhi commented, "If Christians lived according to the teachings of Jesus Christ, there would not be one Hindu left in India."

This bill that is pending before Parliament under the guise of religious freedom is a deception. There is no freedom if a person is not free to choose according to the dictates of his conscience. Our brethren from Arunachal are fearful. Up until now they had lived in peace, but now religious excuses have begun to be used to destroy the love that they have for one another, just because some are Christians. But others are Hindus and still others are Muslims.

Some in our country call God Ishwar. Others call him Allah. And others just call him God. Every one of us has to recognize that he created us for greater things, such as to love and be loved. Who are we to keep our people from looking for God who has created them, who loves them, and to whom we all must return one day?

Gandhi, the father of our country, said, "He who serves the poor serves God." I spend hours and hours helping the poor, the dying, the unwanted, the despised, the lepers, and the insane. I do it because I love God. I know that whatever I do for my brothers it is as if I did it for him. The only motive and joy in my life is to love him and serve him in the oppressed poor, the hungry, the thirsty, the naked, and the homeless. By working this way, I am proclaiming the love and compassion of God for each one of my brothers and sisters who suffers.

Mr. Desai and gentlemen of Parliament, in the name of God, do not destroy the freedom that our people have always had to love and serve God according to their consciences and their beliefs. Do not look down on the Hindu religion, saying that the poor Hindu people sell their religion for a plate of rice. I have a lot of experience, and I have never seen such a thing happen, even though we feed thousands of hungry from every religion and caste. Thousands of them have died in our arms.[3]

I ask you, I beg you, to declare a day of prayer for the entire nation. We Catholics have asked all of our brothers and sisters to observe a day of fasting, prayer, and sacrifice to preserve peace and unity in our country, so that India may continue to enjoy its noble tradition of religious freedom.

I ask you to propose a similar day for all the religious communities in the nation, so that we may live in peace, unity, and love. May we all have hearts overflowing with love as a reflection of God's love. God's love is what can save our families, our country, and the entire world.

TWELVE

The Suffering of Others

In Haiti just as in England, Spain, Italy, or India—there are unhappy people everywhere. Not only because they don't have any bread to eat. No, they hunger for love, understanding, and companionship. They suffer from loneliness, the feeling of being unwanted and rejected, a poverty of the soul. These are the things that can be far worse than being hungry or not having enough material goods.

In Western countries, your countries, I can perceive this in the people I meet. There exists something in common among your poor and the poor in India: the need for happiness and joy in spite of the hardships of life. It is something marvelous that the same call unites us, so that we can together extend Jesus' saving work.

Let's not live distracted lives. Let us know ourselves so that we can better understand our brothers and sisters. If we want to understand those with whom we

---

Mother Teresa spoke these words in Haiti in the summer of 1980. They were taken down in *Bulletin No. 38 of the International Association of Co-workers of Mother Teresa,* in an article entitled, "Mother Teresa's homage of Mrs. Jean-Claude Duvalier."

live, we need to understand ourselves first of all.

Sometimes we see how joy returns to the lives of the most destitute when they realize that many among us are concerned about them and show them our love. Even their health improves if they are sick. After all, was it not Christ himself who said, "Every time you did it to the least of my brethren, you did it to me"? You are not to be indifferent to the suffering of others, but it is meant to deeply affect you.

THIRTEEN

The Gift of Smiling

Q: What attitude should Christians adopt in a country ravaged by a conflict such as the one that afflicts us [in Great Britain]?

A: Christians need to learn to forgive. We have to be forgiven in order to be able to forgive. I believe that if the people in Belfast—just like elsewhere in Bangladesh, Amman, New York, and other places—would forgive each other, world peace would come.

Q: How does one learn to forgive?

A: By knowing that we too need to be forgiven.

Q: Could you verify the need for forgiveness in Belfast?

A: I have seen this in several families that I have visited where someone was murdered or someone died violently. There is no prejudice in these families. I have seen that these families have forgiven and don't hold

---

This interview took place on January 15, 1973 between Mother Teresa and Ralph Rolls. It was recorded for a program entitled *Belief and Life* of the British Broadcasting Corporation (BBC).

any grudges against the ones who killed their sons. I think that is a first step.

Q: Where, besides Belfast, have you been able to open homes with the Missionaries of Charity?

A: We have two homes in Australia: one among the aborigines and another in Melbourne. There we have a home for alcoholics who are dying, and we even have a home for novices on that continent.

Q: In other words, you are already in Australia.

A: We also have a home in Amman, Jordan. The sisters there have a lot of work to do. Last year they were asked to work with the Bedouins. I am under the impression that up until now, no one in that country had worked in such close contact with those people. Also the Palestinian Arabs have been living there for the past twenty years. They have been considered refugees and still are considered so today. They too have come in contact with the work that the sisters are doing. This has helped them to get to know each other better.

Q: Have you been in Amman recently?

A: Yes, I was there last month. I got the impression that things are a little better than last year. One can tell that peace is taking hold little by little. Something very beautiful is happening. The Jordanian people are becoming aware of their responsibility toward the needy. I have the impression that they are going to take things very seriously. We want to begin construction of a home for the elderly and homeless in that city. That is something very beautiful for our people who feel forgotten, because they are far away from their villages. The same answer comes up again: we must be aware of our need to be forgiven for being the cause of such suffering, for which we need forgiveness. Only then will we be able to forgive others. We all need to become more aware that if we are going to love truly, if we really want peace and love to go together, (we can't separate them) we must forgive.

Q: Is it necessary to be a Christian in order to forgive?

A: No, it is not absolutely necessary. Every human being comes from the hand of God, and we all know something of God's love for us. Whatever our religion, we know that if we really want to love, we must learn to forgive before anything else.

Q: We talked about Amman. Where else are the Missionaries of Charity located?

A: The sisters are also in Rome. In England we have two homes. There are also sisters working in Harlem, New York. There are sisters at two different locations in Venezuela. They are also in Tabora. At present they are very busy with the refugees from Burundi, who have flooded in by the thousands after indescribable suffering. The sisters are also on Mauritius Island, and we have forty-two centers in India.

Q: What sort of an impression have you gotten of England during this short visit?

A: It seems to me that in England there is a very great need to know who the poor are. I don't think the English are able to recognize their poor. Since they don't know them, they find it hard to love them and even harder to serve them. It would be different if we could have people meet each other face to face. If some English people could take the place of one of our sisters (just to give you an example) for a while, that would be helpful. If people could get a sense of what it's like to try to find a home for those who are outside dying in the cold, if they could see firsthand how old people are neglected, despised, and abandoned, by nearly everyone, that would be good.

There are people who sleep in the streets of London, people who use makeshift pieces of cardboard and sheets of newspapers to protect themselves. You have people who shiver in the cold and are half frozen in downtown London. No one seems to take the time or the effort to notice these people. The fact that people don't have time for the poor causes the greatest suffering of all. Oh, the terrible loneliness of our elderly living in a small room completely abandoned by family and friends! Not even their neighbors know them by name, nor do they think of even taking them a glass of water. I believe that this is by far the greatest tragedy in the world today. The English should open their hearts to love the poor and lend them a hand by serving them. But they can't do that unless they first know them. Knowledge leads to love and love to service.

Q: What other observations have you made about English society during your visit?

A: Another thing that I sense is that in England people find it hard to take into account the lives of little children, of unborn children, because they are trying to avoid them.

Q: Are you referring to abortion?

A: Yes, that is what I am referring to. People are trying to be free to live their own life by destroying life. For me, this is a painful sign that either the country is so poor that it cannot care for the lives that God has created, or that people are making a tremendous mistake.

Q: Would you prefer that abortion were illegal?

A: I don't want to talk about what should be legal or illegal. I don't think that any human heart should dare to take life, or any human hand be raised to destroy life. Life is the life of God in us. The life of God is present even in the fetus. We don't have even the slightest right to destroy a life, whether it is that of a child, a man, or a woman. It's all the same. I believe that the cry of these children, these ones who are never born because they are killed before they even see the light of day, must offend God greatly.

Q: How could society take care of so many children if all of them were born?

A: Jesus said that we are much more important to his Father than the grass in the field, the sparrows, or the lilies of the field. If he takes care of things such as these, which are only things, how much more would he care for our lives! He will not deceive us. Life is the greatest gift that God has bestowed on human beings. Since human life is created in the image of God, it belongs to him. We have no right to destroy it.

Q: One of the tragic results of the war in Bangladesh

was the raping of young women by the invading Pakistani troops. According to the local laws, those women could not marry and they would have to be practically thrown out of their towns. Victims of desperation, fear, and shame—some of them committed suicide. Others became insane, and many others fled to India. You and your sisters immediately opened homes to shelter them and offer them the care that they needed. When they were able to return to Bangladesh, the sisters went with them, assisting them so that they could return to their towns. They tried to arrange marriages for the women and managed to have the children who were born placed for adoption. This work of love, reconciliation, and rehabilitation was strengthened and supported by the declaration of the prime minister of Bangladesh that those women were to be considered national heroines.

A: This is something uncommon for Muslims and Hindus, because a young woman who has been abused in such a way must be more or less banished from society. But in this case, something different happened as a response to the declaration of the prime minister of Bangladesh. A very different situation came to pass.

Everyone is making huge sacrifices. People from all around have been very generous. They have offered a great deal of aid to Bangladesh by sending goods, money, and construction materials. Also, the people living there are helping out. For example, state employees have agreed to work for only half their pay for a year, so that the country will again be able to sustain itself.

Q: You need a great deal of money and even publicity to keep your work going, don't you?

A: No, I don't need publicity.

Q: You really don't?

A: I'm telling you that I don't.

Q: But your work needs to be made known, doesn't it?

A: Of course. I allow it to be made known.

Q: But you personally don't look for publicity?

A: No.

Q: Why not?

A: Because God's work must be done his way and he has his own ways of making it known. Just look at what has happened worldwide and how the sisters have been welcomed in places where no one knew anything about them: for example, here in England. Look at how they have been welcomed in Belfast where the sisters, in a way, have become part of the local community.[1] They have been warmly welcomed in Harlem, New York where many people find it hard to live or even visit for a while. That's why I have come to believe that it is God himself who is trying to show us that this is his work.

Q: Perhaps this will seem like a strange question so forgive me for asking, is it important to you to be a Catholic?

A: Very much so. It is most important.

Q: Could it be any other way?

A: Not for me. It couldn't be.

Q: It is the only way for . . . ?

A: For each individual, it is according to the grace that God has given that soul.

Q: Then, it isn't important which Christian denomination we belong to?

A: It is important for individuals. If people think and believe that their church is the only way to God, that is the way in which God will come into their lives. If they don't know any other way—if they don't have the least doubt about it—so that they don't feel the need to look further, then this is the way for their salvation. This is the way in which God comes into their lives. But the moment a soul receives grace to desire to know God and the faith better, then he has to look further. If one doesn't look, he goes astray. But God gives each soul that he has created an opportunity to find itself face to face with him, to accept or reject him. This, for me, is the answer.

Q: Is unity among Christians important to you?

A: Very important. Christians are the light for everyone else, for the whole world. If we are Christians, we must look like Christ. We must be like him. This is a conviction that I have deep inside of me. Gandhi said once that if Christians really lived their Christianity, there wouldn't be any Hindus left in India. That is what people expect from us: that we fully live out our Christianity.

Q: What happens then with the followers of other religions such as Islam or Hinduism? Are they blessed by God also? Does God work in their midst also?

A: God has his own ways of working in the hearts of men, and we do not know how close he is to each one. We have no right to condemn, to judge, or to say things that can hurt other people for their beliefs. It is possible that a person has never heard a word about Christianity. Then we do not know how God is revealing himself to that soul, or in what way God is forming it. So who are we to condemn anyone?

Q: Do you mean that it doesn't matter what a person believes?

A: I am not saying that it doesn't matter what a person believes. I believe that God has created each soul, that that soul belongs to God, and that each soul has to find God in its own lifetime and enter into his life. That is what is important. All of us need to seek God and find him.

Q: What is the biggest obstacle that you encounter in your work?

A: Not being holy yet.

Q: What upsets you the most when you travel around the world?

A: Not to be able to fully radiate Christ's love, because God wants those who belong to him to be happy and holy.

Q: In the event that you had to work in a country where you were only allowed to work for the poor under the condition that you renounce your faith and your religion, would you be capable of staying to help the poor? Or would you have to go elsewhere so you could practice your religion?

A: No one can take my religion away from me. They can't prevent me from believing or snatch it away from me. It is something that is inside of me. And if there were no other alternative, if that were the only way that Christ chose to come to those people, then I would stay to serve them. But I would not renounce my faith. I would be willing to lose my life but not my faith.

Q: How can we believe in a good God when there is so much suffering around us?

A: Suffering in and of itself is useless, but suffering which is a share in the passion of Christ is a marvelous gift for human life. The most wonderful of gifts is that we can share in Christ's passion.

Q: How? Is suffering a gift?

A: Yes, and it is a sign of love because it was chosen by the Father to show us that he loved the world by giving up his Son to die for us. In that way, through Christ's life, suffering proved to be a gift, the greatest gift of love, because through his suffering our sins were atoned for.

Q: Our sins?

A: Yes, above all, our sins. That's why we come back to the same thing. If we admit that we are sinners and we need forgiveness, then it will be very easy for us to forgive others. But if I don't admit this, it will be very hard for me to say, "I forgive you" no matter who comes to me.

Q: What should we do when suffering comes to us?

A: Accept it with a smile.

Q: Accept it with a smile?

A: Yes, with a smile, because it is the greatest gift that God gives us.

Q: What? To smile?

A: To smile at God. To have the courage to accept everything that he sends us, and to give to him what he asks of us with a big smile.

FOURTEEN

A Sea of Poverty

Q: You love people that others consider the rejects of humanity. What is the secret that allows you to do this?

A: My secret is very simple: I pray. Through prayer I become one in love with Christ. I realize that praying to him is loving him. That means that I am fulfilling his commandment. Let's not forget what he tells us: "I was hungry and you fed me not." The poor who live in the slums of the world are the suffering Christ. The Son of God lives and dies through them, and through them God shows me his true face. For me, prayer means being united to the will of God twenty-four hours a day, to live for him, through him, and with him.

Q: If Jesus is head of the church, shouldn't the church show a different face and be more exemplary?

A: But, who is the church? You and I. Jesus doesn't need palaces. Only men need them. The church are those who follow him. Following him is something

---

This interview appeared in *Bulletin No. 38* (Fall 1980) *of the International Association of Co-workers of Mother Teresa.* It was attributed, without further detail, to a Dutch radio program.

that I try to do every day. We live surrounded by people who are hungry for love. That is what we need to give them. If everyone was capable of discovering the image of God in their neighbors, do you think that we would still need tanks and generals? Through the years that I have spent working in the slums I have learned that it is precisely the poor who are aware of human dignity. Their biggest problem isn't a lack of money. It is feeling stripped of their right to human dignity and love. Humanity's greatest sin stems from denying the poor their right to human dignity, because human beings measure being human only by the standard of the things they own.

Q: You live surrounded by a sea of poverty. Is there any hope that the tide will turn?

A: Yes, we live surrounded by a sea of poverty and suffering. Nevertheless, this sea can decrease in size. Our work is only a drop in the bucket, but this drop is necessary. It can represent a new beginning every day. It is something that many people scattered around the world can put into practice every day. In any case, it isn't necessary to go to the slums to have a brush with poverty and experience the lack of love in the world. In every family, as well as in families right next door, there is always someone who is suffering. This is something that we all come across.

Q: When will the day come in which the sea of poverty disappears?

A: When all of us recognize that our suffering neighbor is the image of God himself and when we understand the consequences of that truth. That day poverty will no longer exist and we, the Missionaries of Charity, will no longer have any work to do.

Q: If God created the world, why does he allow such a degree of poverty to exist?

A: God created the world and saw that it was good. God created man and saw that he was good. God created everything, and he realized that each thing was good. How can we complain against God for the poverty and suffering that exist in the world? Can we honestly do so? God saw that everything was good. What we do with things is another matter. Let's love one another first of all in India no less than in Europe. That will accomplish miracles.

FIFTEEN

A Lesson from the Poor

Q: Can you somehow summarize your experience with the poor?

A: I have learned from the poor how poor I myself am. They give me infinitely more than I give them: their joy (they are content with everything), their zest for life, their receptiveness, their way of accepting things. What rich person can live daily without food and clothing? There are millions of poor people who can. One day a very rich man came to the home for dying destitutes in Calcutta. Upon departing he said to me, "Now I realize how poor I am." Personally I have to admit that my contact with the poor has completely changed my life. Through them I have understood the

---

Mother Teresa answered these questions at a press conference. (No further details are available.) She said at another one in Spain on June 24, 1980 that if she avoided purgatory, it would be because of the journalists and photographers who have made her suffer purgatory beforehand! If we only had an idea of how hard it is for her to be constantly bombarded with the same questions over and over again, day after day!

unsurpassed power of Jesus' words: "I was hungry and you gave me to eat. I was homeless and you took me in." I have gambled everything with the assurance that Jesus will not disdain me. At the same time, he himself is made poor by becoming our food in the Eucharist. He knows the countless hungers of man, and he gives of himself. What a gift! What proof of his love! What assurance for us!

Q: There are people who criticize you, saying that you place too much emphasis on charity and not enough on justice. What do you have to say?

A: I have already said that we take care of one person. Then if we can, we take care of another. We never cure multitudes. Our particular vocation is to love each person God brings to us today. The vocation to do more long-term work is up to others. Love, tenderness, and compassion are real justice. Justice without love is not justice. Love without justice is not love. Often we hear it said that we pamper our poor too much. No one has pampered them except God himself. It is good that there is at least one religious congregation that pampers the poor. There are more than enough people to pamper the rich.

Q: What motivates you to go from one continent to another? Don't you worry about becoming a bureaucrat of charity?

A: Jesus said, "Go and teach all nations." In every country there are poor. On certain continents poverty is more spiritual than material. That poverty consists of loneliness, discouragement, and the lack of meaning in life. I have also seen in Europe and America very poor people sleeping on newspapers or rags in the streets. There are those kind of poor in London, Madrid, and Rome. My visits have the sole purpose of making people aware of the poor in their own countries. It is too easy simply to talk or concern ourselves with the poor who are far away. It is much harder and, perhaps, more challenging to turn our attention and concern toward the poor who live right next door to us.

Q: Doesn't it make you uncomfortable to find yourself considered a living saint?

A: Each one of us is what he is in the eyes of God. We are all called to be saints. Holiness isn't a luxury reserved for only a few but a simple duty for all of us. There is nothing extraordinary about this call. We all have been created in the image of God to love and to be loved.

Q: What is most essential in the vocation and mission of your sisters?

A: We are not social workers. Our vocation is to belong to Jesus. He has chosen us for himself alone. What we do for the poorest of the poor is nothing more than to put into practice our love for Christ, like a living parable.

Q: What advice would you give to the people of today?

A: Know the poorest of the poor among your neighbors, in your neighborhoods, in your town, in your city, perhaps in your own family. When you know them, that will lead you to love them. And love will impel you to serve them. Only then will you begin to act like Jesus and live out the gospel. Place yourselves at the service of the poor. Open your hearts to love them. Be living witnesses of God's mercy. This may lead you to give up your own sons so that they may serve God, who gives preference to the poor.

Q: Mother Teresa, how is it possible for you to discover Christ under the appearance of alcoholics and drug addicts, as you say you do?

A: None of us has the right to condemn anyone. Even though we see some people doing something bad, we don't know why they are doing it. Jesus invites us to not pass judgment. Maybe we are the ones who have helped make them what they are. We need to realize that they are our brothers and sisters. That leper, that drunkard, and that sick person is our brother because he too has been created for a greater love. This is something that we should never forget. Jesus Christ identifies himself with them and says, "Whatever you did to the least of my brethren, you did it to me." That leper, that alcoholic, and that beggar is my brother. Perhaps it is because we haven't given them our understanding and love that they find themselves on the streets without love and care.

I believe that we should realize that poverty doesn't only consist in being hungry for bread, but rather it is a tremendous hunger for human dignity. We need to love and to be somebody for someone else. This is where we make our mistake and shove people aside. Not only have we denied the poor a piece of bread, but by thinking that they have no worth and leaving them abandoned in the streets, we have denied them the human dignity that is rightfully theirs as children of

God. They are my brothers and sisters as long as they are there. And why am I not in their place? This should be a very important question. We could have been in their place without having received the love and affection that has been given to us. I will never forget an alcoholic who told me his story. He was a man who gave in to drinking so he could forget that he wasn't loved. I think we should examine our own conscience before judging the poor, be they poor in spirit or poor in material goods.

Q: Missionaries used to be sent from the supposedly civilized world to the so-called Third World. Now you are coming from India to evangelize us.

A: It is just what Jesus said, "Go and preach the good news to all nations." Spain is one of the nations where we want to preach. Just as St. Francis Xavier was your gift to India, now India is giving you missionaries prepared by St. Francis Xavier, who are returning and proclaiming the good news. This is a sign of the joy of loving God: sharing that love with others. The joy of loving God should be shared. The best way to love God is for us to love one another as he has loved us. He died on the cross to show us his love. And as if that were not enough for him, he became the Bread of Life to satisfy our hunger for God. Then he even became the hungry so that you and I could satisfy his hunger for us. That is why it is so wonderful to receive the Eucharist and to tend to the poor for the love of Christ.

Perhaps in rich countries people aren't hungry for bread as they are in India or Africa. In India we do have rich people. But I think it is much easier to give a plate of rice or a piece of bread to a hungry person than to

eliminate loneliness, and the feeling of being unwanted—a feeling that many rich people have who
spend their days alone. I think that is great poverty.

Q: You work among the lepers.

A: During the passion, Jesus' face was like the face of a
leper. When I see lepers I think that the passion of
Christ is being re-lived in them. They are wonderful.
They have no bitterness in their lives. At this very
moment we are caring for fifty-three thousand lepers
in India. It is wonderful to see how these people want
to go on living. We are building rehabilitation centers.
They have their own dispensaries and schools. They do
their own work, and they lead a normal life. This has
brought a new life and a new joy to their old lives. This
also makes them feel like beloved children of God.

We also have rehabilitation centers in Yemen where
the government has given us land, in Ethiopia, and in
Tanzania. Wherever the sisters are, the first thing that
we try to do is check out the situation. We find out
where the lepers, the poor, and those who cannot fend
for themselves are. It gives us great joy to be with
them, because this is the passion of Christ made a
reality in our lives.

Q: And you work among the dying.

A: Death is the most decisive moment in human life. It
is like our coronation: to die in peace with God. I have
never seen anyone die desperate or blaspheming. They
all die serenely, almost with joy. A man that I had
rescued from the streets and taken to the home for
dying destitutes said to me, "I have lived like an animal
in the streets, but I am going to die like an angel." And

he died smiling because he was being loved and cared for. That is the greatness of our poor.

Q: How do you administrate the money that you receive in ever increasing amounts?

A: We receive it with our right hand, and we give it away with our left. We don't have fundraising campaigns. We don't need them. We don't even have to beg. We would beg if we had to, but we don't need to because people come to us. Even children help us. We only just arrive in a certain country, and the people are already giving to us. I don't know who they are or where they live, but everywhere the same thing happens. We welcome the poor, and we need to be poor like them if we want to understand them. Our poverty is our strength and our freedom.

Q: What will happen, Mother, when you are no longer with us?

A: I believe that if God finds a person even more useless than me, he will do even greater things through her because this work is his. I am sure that the sisters will work with the same energy. As long as they remain faithful to their poverty and to the Eucharist, they will be faithful to the poor. There is no reason to worry. There is nothing to fear. God has always found someone, just like he found me.

Q: Mother Teresa, haven't you had any regrets in your life?

A: I don't remember any, but if I had to start all over again, I would do the same thing. I have experienced many human weaknesses, many human frailties, and I still experience them. But we need to use them. We need to work for Christ with a humble heart, with the humility of Christ. He comes and uses us to be his love and compassion in the world in spite of our weaknesses and frailties.

SIXTEEN

The Temptation to Change Everything

Doing Ordinary Things with Love

Let us always ask our Lady to be with us when we pray together. Our intercessory prayer to Mary, the mother of Jesus shall be this:

Give us a heart as beautiful, pure, and spotless as yours. A heart like yours, so full of love and humility. May we be able to receive Jesus as the Bread of Life, to love him as you loved him, to serve him under the mistreated face of the poor. We ask this through Jesus Christ our Lord. Amen.

Zachaeus was a rich man, a tax collector, and very well known in the community, the Gospel tells us. He was anxious to see Jesus, but he couldn't see him. His

---

This brief talk was given by Mother Teresa to women religious from different orders and congregations in Holland. It was given during a meeting she had with them in Eindhoven on October 24, 1983. The text was made available by Jan Colenbrander of the International Association of Co-workers of Mother Teresa.

height didn't allow him to. But then he became aware of his shortness. He did what a child would have done. He climbed up a tree. That gesture of humility granted him the grace to see Jesus. Jesus headed towards the tree, and Zachaeus came down when Jesus called to him.

Likewise you and I, who have consecrated our lives to Jesus, should be aware that we are small. We should make a decision to do little things with great love. When Therese of Lisieux[1]—the Little Flower—died and was about to be canonized, everyone was asking, "What reason is there for the Holy Father to canonize her? She hasn't done anything extraordinary." The Holy Father pointed out in writing the reason for his decision: "I want to canonize her because she did ordinary things with extraordinary love."

God Loves Us

Ordinary things with extraordinary love! You see. We also have the opportunity to be canonized one day, since we are only called to do the ordinary, little things of life. As people completely consecrated to Jesus, we have within us an attraction toward humble things, hidden things, the seemingly insignificant things of life.

Jesus, in fact, to show his Father's love for the world, became so small and helpless that he needed a mother to care for him. And Mary felt like a little creature, just like you and me, and found it so natural to say: "Behold the handmaid of the Lord." Yet she had been conceived without sin and was the spotless virgin of our Savior.

In the very instant she surrendered herself completely to the will of God, she was filled with divine grace and with Jesus himself. Without losing any time, she ran to give Jesus to others. It is surprising that she, the very Mother of God, would run to give Jesus to others. She, who was the Mother of God, went in haste to do the work of a servant.

We know, dear brothers and sisters, what wonderful thing happened. Just as she entered the house, the little baby John, yet to be born, leapt for joy. It is surprising how God chose a little unborn baby to proclaim the presence of Christ! Yet today, they are trying to kill unborn babies! Let us ask our Lady to remove from mothers' hearts this horrible temptation, to want to eliminate the child in their wombs.

If we look around us, there seems to be a growing urgency to destroy the life that God has created. This is in spite of the fact that you and I know full well that each little child—these little defenseless children, just like we were once—has been created for greater things: to love and be loved.

The Scriptures tell us, "I have called you by name. You belong to me. You are precious to me. I love you." God himself declares that we are precious to him. He loves us, and he wants us to respond to his love. In a special way, this refers to those of us who have committed ourselves to belong to God. Your vocation, as well as mine, can be summed up this way: to belong to Jesus, to love with the conviction that nothing and no one can ever separate us from the love of Christ. We want to love him with an undivided love through chastity. We want to embrace poverty willingly for him. We want to surrender ourselves freely. We want to give of ourselves generously through obedience and service to the poor.

The Call to Give Jesus to Others

How can we put our undivided love for Christ into action? We do that by serving, by accomplishing what the church has commissioned us to do. As for us in the Missionaries of Charity, we profess a fourth vow to give wholehearted and free service to the poorest of the poor. Because of this vow, we depend totally upon God's providence. We do not accept any monies from the state, any social security, or any ecclesiastical stipend. We do not have salaries, service fees, bank accounts, or fixed incomes of any sort.

Nevertheless, I assure you that the day has yet to come when we have had to tell our needy that we have no resources. There is always something. And that something is God's Word which has promised us that we are more important to him than the lilies, the sparrows, or the grass in the field.

The fruit of our work, as well as the ability to carry it out, comes from prayer. The work that we accomplish is the fruit of our union with Christ. We have been called to give Jesus to the peoples of the world, so that they can look at him and discover his love, his compassion, and his humility in action.

The Temptation to Change

The religious life is going through a period of convulsions today. Believe me, my brothers and sisters in the religious life, everything will turn out all right if we surrender ourselves to God and submit ourselves to him through obedience. Let us obey the church. Let's obey the Holy Father who has a special love for us and truly desires us to be the bride of the crucified Christ.

We see ourselves surrounded by a thousand temptations that go against our vocation and against ourselves. There are so many changes and fads. That is not what is expected of us. Our young people have a burning desire to give themselves completely to God. For that very reason, they are afraid to embrace our way of life. They are afraid that while they are searching for this complete surrender to God, they will discover that is not what we are offering them. Such problems don't only exist in Holland. They exist everywhere. That's why all of us should fall on our knees in the presence of the Blessed Sacrament and pray fervently.

Permit me to give you some advice: begin with the adoration of the Blessed Sacrament as the heart of prayer in your communities. Begin having it weekly, and you will see that soon the young brothers and sisters will ask if you can have it daily. Because as we advance in years, we experience a greater hunger for Jesus. The younger ones will encourage us through their magnificent example of sincere love for Jesus.

The Surest Way to Holiness

We have a great deal of worth in the eyes of God. I never tire of saying over and over again that God loves us. In the Constitution of the Missionaries of Charity, we have a beautiful statement about chastity. It says, "Jesus offers his lifelong, faithful, and personal friendship, embracing us in tenderness and love." It is a wonderful thing that God himself loves me tenderly.

That is why we should have courage, joy, and the conviction that nothing can separate us from the love of Christ.

I receive many applications from many congregations. Many religious from different congregations want to join the Missionaries of Charity. I always tell them, "Truly live according to your rule. You will have no reason to change." Indeed, the constitutions approved by the church have the written Word of God. Therefore, let us ask for the grace to remain faithful to our constitutions and to belong only to Jesus.

Pray for us that we won't spoil the work God has given us to do. As for me, I will pray and ask my sisters to pray for you. We will pray that you may grow in holiness through faithfulness to your rules and constitutions that have been approved by the church for the glory of God. There is no surer way to great holiness. May God bless you!

Chapter Notes

Chapter One
We Will Be Judged by Our Love

1. Anyone who is aware of the spontaneous character of Mother Teresa's words will not be surprised that she often does not quote Scripture word for word. No one would expect such exactness from someone who speaks more from the heart and through her actions than with her words. At the same time, no one can miss the faithful evangelistic paraphrase that she gives of Scripture.

2. Mother Teresa is not condemning nursing homes per se, but rather the increasing tendency to "get rid of old people" because they "are in the way." There will always be some cases in which the elderly will receive better care in a well staffed, caring nursing facility than with their immediate or extended family.

3. Mother Teresa is referring to those who have been students in Catholic schools in the LaSallian Federation.

4. The Missionaries of Charity opened a home in Palermo, Italy on June 9, 1974. Groups of young people from Malta still come during the summer months to this home to assist the sisters in their work.

Chapter Three
Holiness Is Everyone's Duty

1. Mother Teresa always invites her audience to join her in prayer at the beginning of her addresses, especially if the audience is familiar with her work. The most common prayer is the one attributed to St. Francis of Assisi, "Make Me a Channel of Your Peace." On other occasions she recites "The Lord's Prayer." If the gathering is toward evening, she quite often invites her audience to pray the "Angelus" with her.

2. Mother Teresa is referring to the necessary ecclesiastical approval that the Missionaries of Charity have been given. The order was founded on October 7, 1950. At first, diocesan approval was given. In 1965, papal approval was granted, giving the Missionaries of Charity worldwide recognition. A year before final approval was given, Pope Paul VI, an admirer and supporter of Mother Teresa, gave her a white Lincoln convertible that was a gift to him from American Catholics. He had used it during his visit to Bombay (December 2-6, 1964) for the International Eucharistic Congress. The Missionaries of Charity raffled the car off. With the proceeds they started the construction of the Shanti Nagar, a village for several thousand leper families. The Missionary Brothers of Charity were founded in 1963.

Above all, Mother Teresa's deep gratitude to the church stems from her humility and from the strength of the genuinely evangelistic witness that she and her Missionaries of Charity have given.

3. Mother Teresa is not against nursing facilities but rather the attitude that leads to abandonment of the elderly. She sees no social advantage in countries where such institutions are scarce or non-existent. In those countries, being abandoned by the family and the larger society, which is prejudiced against the elderly, also occurs sometimes.

4. In the beginning of the 1980s, the Missionaries of Charity had homes outside of India in the following countries: Argentina (3), Australia (3), Bangladesh (5), Brazil (2), Spain (2), Ethiopia (2), Germany (3), Ireland (3), Chile (6), Guatemala (6), Israel (6), Italy (6), Jordan (2), Kenya (2), Lebanon (20), Mauritius Islands (2), Mexico (2), Holland (2), Panama (2), Papua New Guinea (3), Peru (2), Philippines (2), Tanzania (3), United States (3), Venezuela (5), Haiti (2), Yemen (3), and Yugoslavia (2). As for the rate of the founding of new homes, in 1979, thirteen were built in India: Rajkot,

Silchar, Shembakkam, Guvalior, Chellanam, Bhilai, Saharanpur, Aurangabad, Katihar, Nalgonda, Shanti Dan, Terpur, Dibrugarh. Thirteen were built outside of India: Reggio, Calabria, Corato, and Ragusa (Italy), Essen (Germany), Zagreb (Yugoslavia), St. Louis and Detroit (United States), Toluca (Mexico), Nairobi (Kenya), Chimbote (Peru), San Salvador da Bahia (Brazil), Sanfil (Haiti), and Kisali (Ruanda).

In 1975, for the silver jubilee of the founding of the Missionaries of Charity, Mother Teresa proposed and met the goal of opening twenty-five new centers for the sisters. When the twenty-fifth center was opened, she said, "From this very moment we are committed to Jesus to prepare for the golden jubilee. She also had in mind another fiftieth anniversary, her fiftieth year as a religious sister, which was celebrated on May 24, 1981. Precisely fifty years before she had made her final vows as a sister of Our Lady of Loreto. She made her vows in Spain after completing her novitiate in Darjeeling, India.

5. This title almost coincides with the mission Mother Teresa has charged her sisters to fulfill: "to be carriers of Christ's love in the slums."

Chapter Five
Children of God: Our Brothers and Sisters

1. According to the Hindu caste system, the lowest and most despised of the social castes are the "untouchables." They are avoided and shunned by the other castes who do not want to be "contaminated" by these undesirables. The "untouchables" are supposed to resign themselves to their misfortune which is deserved due to the disorderly life they led in a previous existence. By accepting their present situation, they believe that they will be able to enjoy a better life in the next reincarnation.

Chapter Six
God Loves Us

1. The young postulant or novice mentioned was from Mauritius Island, according to other versions that Mother Teresa has given of the incident. It is helpful to notice that she varies in the degree of detail given to incidents. She adapts them to the audience at hand. Mother Teresa is usually very brief in her anecdotes and repeats some of them frequently. This is especially pronounced when a number of her talks are presented in the same book, even though the talks were given in different places and on different dates. The repetitious nature of her talks is justifiable, since they deal with basic themes for Christian living. As such they deserve repeating.

2. If the reader pays close attention, it will be evident that Mother Teresa and her interviewer have different perspectives. The question is abstract. It deals with how to eliminate poverty. Her answer is concrete: you share what you have with poor people. Mother Teresa's perspective is personal: she highly values the individual, the human person. She has said that she never thinks in terms of multitudes but of individual persons.

3. A parallel source—an eye witness account of this event—states that this incident occurred in London on Christmas Eve of 1968, which is more than ten years earlier. Mother Teresa says that it occurred "some weeks ago." The discrepancy suggests that the exact dates of certain events are of little importance to Mother Teresa. What is important to her is that the events be classic examples of situations that occur among the sisters. Therefore, they can be illustrative in talks, taking on the nature of parables without losing their historic value.

4. In Mother Teresa's biographies this is mentioned. When Mother Teresa (Agnes Bojaxhiu) was eighteen years of age, she decided to join the Sisters of Our Lady of Loreto, popularly known as the "Irish Ladies." She followed the spiritual guidance and advice of a Jesuit from her home town in making this choice. She entered

the mother house at Rathfarnham (near Dublin) where she stayed for two months. She was then sent to Darjeeling, India. These events occurred in 1929.

Chapter Seven
Giving Is Sharing

1. This last general meeting or convocation of the Missionaries of Charity was not really the last. At the end of 1979, the Missionaries of Charity held another one, at which the innovation mentioned here was ratified.

2. The Missionaries of Charity continue to grow in numbers at a rapid rate.

3. The house of the Missionaries of Charity in Rome is the home for novices from all over Europe. For a few years it was the home for novices from all countries, except India. Now there are homes for novices in Africa, the United States, and Australia.

4. Even though the exact number of co-workers of Mother Teresa cannot be accurately known, it is worth noting that at the beginning of the 1980s it was estimated that there were 100,000, of which 80 percent were non-Catholic. A few years later Mother Teresa said that there were 250,000-300,000 co-workers.

5. The Missionaries of Charity are growing at a rate of about two hundred novices per year. This should be taken into account when estimating the present number. By 1984 there were over two thousand, according to the congregation.

6. This meeting took place on August 14-16, 1976 in Lippstadt, West Germany.

7. The words that seem to have been misinterpreted were the ones in an address by Mother Teresa in Lippstadt, West Germany, in August of 1976. They were published in a newsletter by Ann Blaikie, chairman of the International Co-workers of Mother Teresa. "We depend upon God's providence, and I do not want people to get the idea that we are out looking for their money. I do not

want us to give the impression of being a group of men, women, and children who have the goal of getting the most possible money out of people. That is the last thing that would occur to me. I want it to also be the last thing that occurs to you. We should not give that impression, nor should we worry about how much we manage to collect, invest, or have in the bank. Co-workers must also depend upon God's providence and not act independently. If people give, praise God. But, please avoid taking on regular projects which take up your time in fundraising. I do not allow it in India and I would prefer that you not do it here. I do not want you to ask people to make regular, weekly, or monthly contributions. I prefer that you spend your time really serving the needy."

8. This is one of the welfare centers that the Missionaries of Charity have in Rome. It was formerly a monastery run by the Carmaldolese Monks. They put it at Mother Teresa's disposal for her works of charity among the poor.

9. Some feathers were ruffled when Mother Teresa sought the assistance of City Hall in Rome, but her proposal was to bring about a beneficial social program. That is what counts in the last analysis when dealing with public officials or their agents.

10. This occurred two days before Mother Teresa received an honorary degree of Doctor of Divinity at the University of Cambridge.

Chapter Eight
The Poor Are Rich in Love

1. Brother Andrew is the General Servant of the Missionary of Charity Brothers. His title is derived from the gospel understanding that his responsibility—as head of a men's order—entails the call to be a servant, giving wholehearted and free service to the poorest of the poor.

2. Besides not being an "historian" in the strict sense, Mother Teresa tends not to be very exact when giving dates. The dramatic events in Bangladesh actually oc-

curred in 1970-1972. The fact that Mother Teresa shows little regard for precise dates suggests that she considers each event as something of recent occurrence. Just so she is convinced that charity and love for the poor is something that is always in the present and not in the past. It should impel us forward every moment of our lives.

3. Mother Teresa is basing her calculations from the time of the official founding of the Missionaries of Charity on October 7, 1950.

Chapter Nine
Smiling at Christ in His Poor

1. 1979 was declared the International Year of the Child by the United Nations.

2. It is not clear what Mother Teresa is grateful for. It may be the money that was raised by the Norwegian people, aside from the Nobel Peace Prize. Perhaps it was the prize itself or something else. Her companions were Sisters Agnes and Gertrude, Ann Blaikie, Jacqueline de Decker, along with co-worker chairmen from England, Malta, France, Italy, Germany, Denmark, Sweden, Holland, the United States, and Switzerland.

3. The social and geographical context of the talk should be taken into account: Oslo, Norway. The standard of living in the Scandinavian countries is among the highest in the world. Nevertheless, Mother Teresa's words come from her personal conviction that poverty doesn't exclusively consist in the deprivation of material goods.

4. The Missionary of Charity Brothers have a similar rule to that of the Missionaries of Charity. However, their biblical testimony of charity is even more radical. Brother Andrew, an ex-Jesuit from Australia, heads the order as its general servant.

5. Mother Teresa's final words, "God bless you," always end any public pronouncement, whether spoken or written by Mother Teresa or her sisters.

Chapter Ten
The Joy and Freedom of Poverty

1. Mother Teresa is referring to her initiative of pairing a contemplative religious community with a community of the Missionaries of Charity, so that they may offer intercessory prayer for each other.

2. Mother Teresa gives special preference to her sick and handicapped co-workers, each of whom offers their sufferings for a particular Sister of Charity. The sister, in turn, prays for that sick person. It is a gesture of intimate spiritual sharing to which Mother Teresa attaches great importance. She herself established this practice of spiritual solidarity when she accepted Jacqueline de Decker, an ex-missionary from Belgium, as her "sponsor" when her congregation was first founded. Jacqueline de Decker has suffered numerous surgeries and is almost completely paralyzed. She is International Chairman for the Sick and Suffering Co-workers of Mother Teresa. Her address is: Karmel Ooms Straat 14, 1018 Antwerp, Belgium.

3. Mother Teresa cites some of the most well-known examples of children's donations. It should be noted, however, that schoolchildren in other countries also make donations to Mother Teresa's work among poor children.

4. Mother Teresa is asking for vocations for her Missionaries of Charity, but she is also implying that she desires men and women for the church in general and the Missionary of Charity Sisters and Brothers in particular.

5. Hyderabad is the capital of Andhra Pradesh, a state located in the south-central region of India, and has a population of over two million.

6. Imperial Chemical Industries is an important international company which manufactures a wide range of chemical products.

7. The religious congregation of the Missionary of Charity Brothers was founded on March 25, 1963, and inspired by the rule and charitable goals of Mother Teresa's work.

It is, however, independent of the Missionaries of Charity. Besides being established in India, the brothers are also found in numerous other countries, several of their houses are in the Americas. Their way of life, dedicated to serving the poor, is even more radically biblical than that of the sisters.

8. This special branch of the Missionaries of Charity is called the Missionary Sisters of the Word. It was established in New York on the feast day of the Sacred Heart in June 1976. The new branch received the blessing of the late Cardinal Terence Cooke. There is also a small parallel branch called the Brothers of the Word, which should not be confused with the congregation headed by Brother Andrew. The Brothers of the Word work directly under the authority of Mother Teresa.

9. White is the color of mourning in India, just the opposite of Western usage. By choosing white saris with a blue border for the Sisters of Charity and all-white for the Missionary Sisters of the Word, Mother Teresa chose colors that are very familiar among the poor.

Chapter Eleven
True Religious Freedom

1. At the time of this letter, the prime minister was eighty-two years of age.

2. This proposed law, which never passed in Parliament, proved to be the downfall of the prime minister. It would have prohibited "converting anyone through coercion, deceit, or any incentive." It would have given the police a pretext to investigate the motives of those who converted someone to another religion.

3. The prime minister even accused Mother Teresa of obligating her schoolchildren, her orphans, and the poor who died in her care to become Christians. This forced her to take an active stand against the proposed law. It did not have merely political implications. It constituted a personal attack on her and the order.

Chapter Thirteen
The Gift of Smiling

1. The home of the Missionaries of Charity in Belfast has been one of the few (possibly the only one) that had to close soon after it was opened, apparently for reasons beyond the sisters' control. While they were in Belfast, the sisters shared courageously in the dangers that the rest of the population endured.

Chapter Sixteen
The Temptation to Change Everything

1. St. Thérèse of the Child Jesus, the canonized name of Thérèse of Lisieux, is the saint Mother Teresa chose as her protectress. On more than one occasion she has said, "My name doesn't come from Teresa the Great (of Avila) but from the little Thérèse."

Also available in Fount Paperbacks

Mother Teresa: Her People and Her Work
DESMOND DOIG

'Desmond Doig has written a beautiful book and his writing and the pictures capture Mother Teresa and her people and her work exactly. He understands it. I want to cry, with anger, with passion, with compassion, with sadness at the waste of human life and energy. But no, that is not enough, it is a waste of energy, we must do something to help her.'

Financial Times

Something Beautiful for God
MALCOLM MUGGERIDGE

'For me, Mother Teresa of Calcutta embodies Christian love in action. Her face shines with the love of Christ on which her whole life is centred. *Something Beautiful for God* is about her and the religious order she has instituted.'

Malcolm Muggeridge

A Gift for God
MOTHER TERESA

'This selection of Mother Teresa's sayings, prayers, meditations, letters and addresses on themes of love and compassion . . . touches profound spiritual themes . . . Its size belies its power to inspire and uplift.'

Church of England Newspaper

The Love of Christ
MOTHER TERESA

A further collection of Mother Teresa's writings and sayings, including hitherto unpublished extracts from her retreat addresses to her community of nuns.

'Do not read this book . . . if you do not want . . . to be shaken in conscience and shamed into loving God and other people more.'

Iain Mackenzie, Church Times

Fount Paperbacks

Fount is one of the leading paperback publishers of religious books and below are some of its recent titles.

- [ ] FRIENDSHIP WITH GOD David Hope   £2.95
- [ ] THE DARK FACE OF REALITY Martin Israel   £2.95
- [ ] LIVING WITH CONTRADICTION Esther de Waal   £2.95
- [ ] FROM EAST TO WEST Brigid Marlin   £3.95
- [ ] GUIDE TO THE HERE AND HEREAFTER
                              Lionel Blue/Jonathan Magonet   £4.50
- [ ] CHRISTIAN ENGLAND (1 Vol) David Edwards   £10.95
- [ ] MASTERING SADHANA Carlos Valles   £3.95
- [ ] THE GREAT GOD ROBBERY George Carey   £2.95
- [ ] CALLED TO ACTION Fran Beckett   £2.95
- [ ] TENSIONS Harry Williams   £2.50
- [ ] CONVERSION Malcolm Muggeridge   £2.95
- [ ] INVISIBLE NETWORK Frank Wright   £2.95
- [ ] THE DANCE OF LOVE Stephen Verney   £3.95
- [ ] THANK YOU, PADRE Joan Clifford   £2.50
- [ ] LIGHT AND LIFE Grazyna Sikorska   £2.95
- [ ] CELEBRATION Margaret Spufford   £2.95
- [ ] GOODNIGHT LORD Georgette Butcher   £2.95
- [ ] GROWING OLDER Una Kroll   £2.95

All Fount Paperbacks are available at your bookshop or newsagent, or they can be ordered by post from Fount Paperbacks, Cash Sales Department, G.P.O. Box 29, Douglas, Isle of Man. Please send purchase price plus 22p per book, maximum postage £3. Customers outside the UK send purchase price, plus 22p per book. Cheque, postal order or money order. No currency.

NAME (Block letters) _____

ADDRESS_____

_____

_____